Valley of
A Hundred Chapels

Yorkshire non-conformists'
lives and legacies

We love the veneral

Our fathers built to God,

In heaven are kept their grateful vows,

Their dust endears the sod.

From humble tenements around,

Came up the pensive train,

And in the Church a blessing found

Which filled their homes again.

Ralph W. Emerson, 1833.

Published by Grace Judson Press, Heptonstall.

For Ian, who is very keen on enthusiasm.

Below: A Mount Zion Primitive Methodist Church tableau for a procession through Mytholmroyd in 1914. The name of the cart is Joah Crossland, house furnisher, Mytholmroyd.

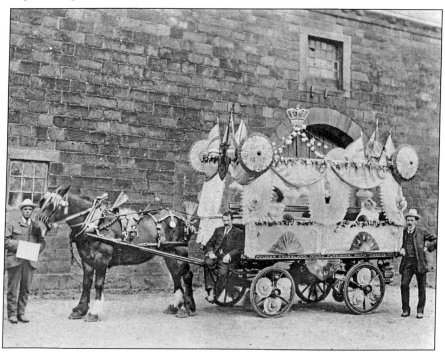

Contents

Part One

4   Rebels and Pioneers

15   Growing Confidence

28   Tea and a Good Sing

40   Sunday Schools

49   Sons of Poverty Assemble

56   A Homely Spirituality

64   Women Find a Voice

72   The Fall of Zion

Part Two

79   Finding our Legacies

90   Reading a Chapel

91   Bethels and Ebenezers

93   Acknowledgements

Chapter One
Rebels and Pioneers

The chapels of today, with their associations of teetotalism and Victorian values, seem the epitome of dull respectability. They are a million miles from the flamboyance of Roman Catholicism, and without the political clout of the "Establishment on its knees" in the Church of England.

But for two centuries, they were firebrand breakaways from the state-sponsored church whose very names – "non-conformist" and "dissenter" - showed their refusal to accept the status quo.

Their members included crusaders and political agitators at a time of huge social change, and their messages of independence and human rights found great resonance with the impoverished Northern weavers, millworkers and smallholders.

Much of what we now accept as truisms about chapel-goers is based on propaganda by the Victorian establishment, including "respectable" authors such as Dickens and Robert Browning, who were horrified by the social revolution happening in every town and village.

But nowhere did the flame burn brighter than in these narrow valleys and windswept hills, all but forgotten by the Church of England and ripe for the seeds of change.

The first of these seeds blew in with travelling preachers, who found the Upper Calder Valley a wild and even brutal place. Due to its difficult terrain, few people were regular churchgoers and even fewer had enough schooling to read the Bible for themselves.

Before the mills arrived, the people were too poor to provide a wealthy living for a gentleman minister, and consequently were largely neglected by the Church of England. The nearest vicar was in Halifax, with curates at chapels-of-ease in Luddenden, Sowerby Bridge, Sowerby, Heptonstall and Cross Stone in Todmorden. Even these were sometimes left without any priest for months. For most of the parishioners, spread out on farms with only packhorse tracks crossing muddy valleys, the nearest Sunday service was simply too far away. At best, only about nine per cent of residents could be classed as communicants of the Church of England.

In this vacuum, new forms of worship could grow. The principles these groups followed were not particularly original: the idea that ordinary people could and should read the Bible themselves to communicate directly with God, without the need of an intermediary priest or state Church, went back to the beginnings of Protestantism in the 1500s.

But the British authorities had never been sure they liked the idea of gifting any form of independence to the masses. They vacillated with whomever was in power, becoming strictly Puritan under Oliver Cromwell and then swinging back to a state Church with the Restoration of Charles II. In an attempt to crack down on the remnants of Cromwell's Puritanism, Par-

Oliver Heywood (1630-1702) was said to have travelled 1,400 miles and preached 105 times, not including Sundays, in a single year. He was imprisoned for 11 months in York castle but was released and carried on preaching. He is buried in Halifax Church. This 19th century painting is based on earlier engravings. Collection: Mansfield College, University of Oxford.

liament unintentionally fanned the flames by passing stricter laws on forms of worship, the 1662 Uniformity Act. Now, breaking away from the Church of England's proscribed forms of worship meant breaking the law. So many ministers felt they were unable to comply in good conscience that hundreds left the church, gifting the movement educated, experienced leaders.

Forbidden by law to go within five miles of their previous churches, homeless and with a constant threat of imprisonment, they naturally became evangelists. Willing to wander amongst their flocks and share their poverty, they brought a personal and dynamic Christianity to remote communities for the first time.

One was Oliver Heywood, a Northowram minister who visited the Calder valley many times, speaking at Sowerby and Cross Stones, and leading meetings at Great House Farm, Eastwood. In his diaries he wrote that after preaching at Stiperden, on the Long Causeway above Todmorden, his host Nathaniel Sutcliffe had nothing to offer but toasted oat bread and butter, served on the only trencher he possessed, with two pennyworth of ale from the inn next door. But despite the remoteness, he recorded:

"God sent abundance of people many miles, tho' it was in the night and very dark and slippery, it did me good to see such a willingness, God affected my heart with poor ignorant soules sad condition in the want of powerfull preaching. I struggled with them in my Lord's name 3 houres that night till I was tired and very hoarse."

At one illegal meeting in 1683 before a large crowd near Cross Stone chapel, above Todmorden, his sermon was interrupted by Major Marshall, who was in the awkward position of being both deputy constable for the dissenting Quaker John Fielding, and a clerk at the Church of England Cross Stone Chapel, where he was friends with the curate Richard Robinson. Heywood cut short his sermon – which had already lasted two hours – but Major Marshall didn't seem overkeen to pursue the matter. It seemed

The Sowerby Street meeting house is Grade 2 listed. Though a little dilapidated, the date stone is still visible reading ISS 1679, standing for Joshua Smith, Sowerby. The distinctive doorway is known as ogee-arched, with an carving on the left.

clear he had been put up to it by the curate Robinson, who had announced a sermon at his own chapel on the same day, to which no-one had come.

The Quakers, or Society of Friends, who refused to bear arms, pay tithes or take oaths, had a hard time of it. Members of their Mankinholes group, who met at each others' houses, were regularly fined large sums or had their goods seized in lieu of tithes.

It was sometimes possible to buy your way out of trouble. The first records of a purpose-built non-conformist chapel, aside from the many house meetings, are at Sowerby. Joshua Horton Esq, JP, of Sowerby Hall, and several other prominent families visited Oliver Heywood, whose cause they wanted to join, in 1672. Mr Horton then built his own non-conformist meeting house in Quarry Hill (exact location unknown), with services held on Tuesdays. However, he sweetened the bitter pill for the Sowerby curate Mr Bowker by continuing to attend his CofE services on most Sundays and, more significantly, giving him £8 per annum, plus an extra 10 shillings for every service held in his own meeting house.

Sowerby Quaker Joshua Smith, who built the Friends chapel still standing on nearby Sowerby Street in 1679, was not so lucky. Oliver Heywood's diaries record that he was arrested and sent to York Castle, along with two other men, for refusing to take a churchwarden's oath. They were told to pay a fine of £8 each for their release, but finally agreed on £6 each.

Despite these setbacks, the non-conformist movement had taken off. Faced with dynastic problems and a divided church, new sovereigns William and Mary chose to accept the inevitable with dignity. The Act of Toleration was passed in 1689 and the first dissenter chapels could be safely built under licence, most of which are still standing. They were modest, due to a lack of funds and perhaps also a lingering fear of drawing official attention.

One of the first was another Quaker house, built in 1694 by the Mankinholes group at nearby Shoebroad and later demolished. The burial ground can still be seen where Shoebroad Lane bends around a clump of trees.

At the same time, two young Heptonstall men began careers as itinerant preachers. William Mitchell, born 1662, and his cousin David Crossley, born 1669, had been brought up together by a devout aunt in what was then "the wildest part of the parish of Halifax".

Crossley "received a saving impression of Gospel truth before he was 12" and grew up to be a 20-stone giant, known as the largest man in the county, who could preach a sermon with 97 separate sections by the time he was 22. Mitchell was a wilder youth, but when he was 19 lost a close relative and had a change of heart.

The Baptist chronicler Dr Parry later wrote of him: "Destitute of high-class culture, rude of speech and of unpolished manners he may have been; yet he was not without natural abilities... he had drunk deep of the spirit of the Gospel. These, combined with great natural force of character, indomitable will, and abounding energy, are sufficient to account for the remarkable power of his preaching."

Crossley's diaries tell how they preached on both sides of the Pennines "through miles in dark nights and over dismal mountains", building up a substantial following. Their supporters licensed some 20 houses in East Lancashire and the West Riding, with a base in Bacup. These meant they could preach without fear of arrest, but these were simply supporters' homes.

Their first purpose built chapel was at Rodwell End, on the hillside to the North West of Todmorden, opened in 1703. It was followed in 1717 by

Rodwell End. It passed to a Methodist group before closing, the Baptists moving down the hill to Millwood. A farmer enlarged one window to make a wider door, causing one wall and the roof to collapse. It is now being restored, one of the original arched windows has been moved up on the left to create a second storey.

a converted barn in Slack, above Heptonstall. The community worshipped alternately in the two chapels. Mitchell died two years after the opening of Rodwell End. A later minister at Slack, E.G.Thomas, wrote: "Measured by figures on a dial, his life was short, for he was only 43 at the time of his death; but measured by intensity of soul, sublimity of purpose, and grandeur of achievement, it was a life beautifully rounded off and complete."

Crossley survived another 39 years, dying a "triumphant and happy" death while pastor at Goodshaw, just over the Lancashire border, a gem of a chapel now owned by English Heritage.

At the same time, a separate group meeting at Great House Farm decided to build Bent Head, Eastwood, which is also still standing as a row of cottages. It remained in use until 1807 when it was replaced by Naze Chapel further down the hill, itself later replaced by Nazebottom in the valley, a nice illustration of how the population shifted as the growing mills needed labour.

The Bent Head design contrasts with the usual C of E and Roman Catholic designs which typically put the entrance in or near the West gable end, with a central aisle leading to an altar at the East. The non-conformists rarely used altars and scorned as superstition the idea that churches had to face a certain way, as God was everywhere. The broad-fronted, double-door design became commonly used for chapels, though it had the disadvantage that latecomers had to scuttle in under the gaze of the whole congregation.

Though they were galleried, the interiors were probably not glowing with the well-polished oak and brass we see in chapels today.

The first Congregational Chapel, opened a little later in 1720 in Sowerby, was "an exceedingly modest building. There was only one pew, that was square in shape with green cushions, and was occupied by a Mr Lea... The rest of the people sat on benches. The ground floor was neither flagged nor boarded, and for their own comfort the people furnished matted straw, or a rug or mat, on which to put their feet."

The gallery was so low that in 1812 the floor was lowered by 18 inches, which must have made it even damper. Later the exterior walls were raised to elevate the roof. After numerous other alterations it was replaced with a Gothic building.

The non-conformist movement was now firmly established, though not a fast-growing force. According to a 1743 religious census, Rodwell End had about 50 worshippers every Sunday, Benthead 130, Stone Slack 30 and the Shoebroad Quakers 100.

But now, free from official intimidation, more wandering preachers appeared, often powerful and charismatic characters. In the absence of formal societies, there were few restrictions on flamboyant individuals. The stages may have been modest, but there were no limits on the performance. This was the era of personalities.

Two men stood out, very different in background and style but both huge in impact: William Grimshaw and William Darney.

Grimshaw was a Cambridge graduate and anointed priest of the Church of England. He was appointed curate to Todmorden in 1731, moving to Haworth in 1746. But despite his establishment background, he felt the

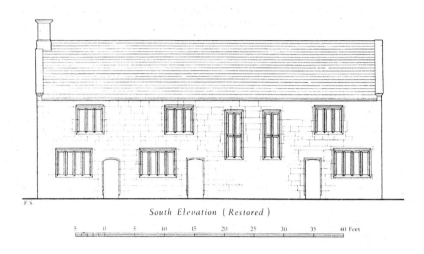

South Elevation (Restored)

Top: Architectural historian Christopher Stell's measured drawing of Bent Head shows how it would originally have looked. At the West end is a small cottage (incorporating cottages next to or below meeting houses became a common way of raising funds through rents). The rest of the meeting house is symmetrical, with two doors and a pair of tall "pulpit" windows, which would have flanked the pulpit standing against the front wall. The upper windows would have lit a gallery at each end, probably joined by a cross gallery at the back. It would have seated about 500 people. Above: Bent Head as it is today, with a new door on the far right, the original right-hand door has been turned into a window. The two long windows have been partly filled in the middle to allow for two storeys.

William Grimshaw, vicar of Haworth. Ted Hughes wrote of him: "To judge by the shock-wave that can still be felt ... he struck the whole region like a planet ... To a degree, he changed the very landscape. His heavenly fire, straight out of Blake's Prophetic Books, shattered the terrain into biblical landmarks; quarries burst open like craters, and chapels – the bedrock transfigured – materialised, standing in them."

power of the evangelicals and threw himself into the new movement. His preaching attracted crowds of "weeping and roaring sinners" trembling at the wrath of God. He frequently visited the valley and influenced the building of the first Wainsgate chapel in 1750, and the original Crimsworth Dean chapel in a converted barn attached to Cross Ends Farm, Haworth Old Road, in 1760.

In contrast, Darney was a pedlar, walking the scattered settlements on the packhorse routes with his pack of handkerchiefs and stockings on his back, preaching and reciting his own poetry as he went. He was described as "a man of prodigious size, and, when he chose, of a terrific countenance... a man possessing few personal attractions, of a broad Scottish dialect, and, when dwelling on the terrors of the Lord, terrible to behold; but a man of deep piety, strong sense and burning zeal." By sheer force of personality, Darney managed to establish a whole series of societies in Gauxholme, near Todmorden, Walsden, Shore and Cross Stone.

When John Wesley and his brother Charles began visiting the valley in 1747, they found much of the groundwork had already been done and the main task was organising and encouraging. The Wesleys did not wish to break with the Church of England – Grimshaw himself was still a C of E curate – but the incumbent priests were suspicious all the same and there was conflict.

Robert Hargreaves, curate of Todmorden, denounced the Methodists as "rogues and knaves and scabbed sheep". John Wesley noted in his 1752 diary (perhaps with some satisfaction) that Hargreaves "was slowly recov-

ROBERTSHAW FARM.
THE OLD PARTICULAR BAPTIST MEETING HOUSE.

Photo by C. E. Pressdee

Top: Stone Slack today. It was bought by the pastor of Rodwell End and Stone Slack congregations, Thomas Greenwood, in 1711, and built on the end of an older barn still standing on the right. The bottom picture shows another barn just visible on the left, since demolished. The area in front was a burial ground, but all trace of this had disappeared by 1900. Now known as Robertshaws, it is only yards from its magnificent later replacement (page 17) at the junction of Widdop Road and Smithwell Lane. Bottom photograph by C.E Pressdee, courtesy of Margaret Morgan.

ering from a violent fit of the palsy, with which he was struck immediately after he had been preaching a virulent sermon against the Methodists."

It would be unfair to tar all the C of E ministers with the same brush. Some invited the Wesleys to speak in their churches, notably at the now ruined St Thomas a Becket church, Heptonstall, which John Wesley rather ungratefully labelled "the ugliest church I know". For their part, the Wesleys insisted that chapels should not compete with churches, and meetings should not clash with C of E service times.

But though some pulpits were open to them, their diaries show they often preached in the open air before huge crowds. The Wesleys were powerful preachers and, together with the locals, successfully led a huge dissenter revival. After a visit to Mankinholes, John Wesley wrote in his diary:

"The people stood, row above row, on the side of the mountain. They were rough enough in outward appearance; but their hearts were as melting wax."

Soon it was decided to build a chapel in Heptonstall. The octagon shape was then fashionable, as the shape made clear that it was not a church, and so avoided conflict with the establishment. For the same reason, they were originally called meeting or preaching houses, and were only later called chapels and still later churches, the terms being used interchangeably.

Heptonstall's was the fourth to be built, many others followed but few have survived. Wesley preached in the unfinished shell, lining out his then unpublished verse, perhaps inspired by the sight of Hardcastle Crags from the hilltop:

> "Ye mountains and vales, in praises abound,
> Ye hills and ye dales, continue the sound,
> Break forth into singing, ye trees of the wood,
> For Jesus is bringing lost sinners to God."

Local historians Chapman and Turner later wrote: "Wesley had obviously been impressed by the roof at the Rotherham Octagon, he had the same man construct the roof in Heptonstall. The sections were brought by the most direct, though hazardous, road over Mount Skip, the people meeting the procession of pack horses and singing hymns of joy. Men and women laboured with their hands to build the chapel with the most primitive of tools."

The building was finished in 1764 and two years later John Wesley returned to preach in it again. How many are privileged to be present at the birth of a great movement? And how many recognise the wings of the angels as they pass over them? In their writings, these fortunate few did not just hope, they had an unshakeable belief which filled them with joy and passion.

But though there was joy, there was not harmony. Throughout the 18th century, much concern was given to doctrinal issues. One of the biggest divides was over infant baptism, with those believing in adult baptism (sometimes called believers' baptism) forming the Baptist societies in contrast to other groups. As the Wesleyans grew in popularity, many new Methodist societies were formed but some dissenters remained independent, and others became Congregationalists. These had no church hierar-

HEPTONSTALL CHAPEL IN 1764.

The engraving, top, shows Heptonstall chapel as originally built, a symmetrical octagon seating 200 with a central arched doorway. By 1802 there were 337 members and 1,002 scholars, proof of the immediate popularity of Sunday schools. The solution was to knock down the far end of the chapel, lengthen the walls and rebuild it, preserving the octagon shape. The arched entrance was partially blocked to form a stained glass window. The adjacent windows were turned into the twin doorways so beloved of the dissenters. By 1821 it was again too small, but this time new chapels were built in Hebden Bridge (Salem), and in Blackshaw Head.

Dan Taylor was born to poor parents in Northowram in 1738. At the age of three he could read well, and at five had to join his father working in a coal pit. At 14 he was preaching for the Wesleyans in Halifax but, after religious arguments, became a Baptist. In 1763, he preached to a congregation of four people gathered under a tree in Nook, Wadsworth. This was the first Birchcliffe congregation.

chy, with each church running its affairs independently.

These groups did not always remain distinct. The charismatic miner's son Dan Taylor was a Methodist preacher but gradually lost faith in the Wesleys and started the Baptist congregation that would become Birchcliffe. Sometimes entire congregations changed sides, and sometimes meeting houses were handed over one group to another – Rodwell End was Methodist for a time. Sometimes the groups worked together – Grimshaw in particular was a peacemaker - but sometimes they tried to undermine each other in very un-Christian ways. After one visit to Todmorden, Charles Wesley wrote that the local Baptists were "a carnal, cavilling, contentious sect, always watching to steal away our children, and make them as dead as themselves".

There were disagreements within congregations, and the arguments over interpretations of Scripture and power struggles may seem archaic or trivial now. These many splits are part of the reason why the valley had so many chapels, such as the row over whether it was right to install an organ which split the tiny Methodist congregation of Mankinholes, resulting in a new Methodist chapel only two fields away at Lumbutts.

This book does not intend to deal with these doctrinal issues, or give a history of the many factions. It would be tedious to the modern reader and paint a false picture of a movement constantly at war with itself.

And these battles were not part of a war. In fact, they were the first rehearsals for a democratic society. For the first time, the working classes were masters of their own meeting houses and schools, learning to read, to make up their own minds and act on their convictions. With growing confidence, in the chapels they had built with their own hands, the working classes learnt to orate, debate and decide. No wonder the establishment trembled.

Chapter Two
Growing Confidence

In the 18th century as never before, change was in the air. The French uprisings even before the revolution had brought ideas of *liberté, égalité, fraternité,* and some historians claim the sudden rush of energy was not just a Christian revival, but a Methodist revolution.

In the Upper Calder Valley, ten chapels had been formed in the 70 years to 1764. In the next 70 years, another 30 were opened. These included the first Todmorden chapel in Doghouse Lane in 1784, the graceful Georgian Mount Zion Chapel in Upper Brockholes in 1815, and chapels in Luddenden, Mankinholes and Sowerby Bridge

These chapels were not just meant for worship, they were nerve centres of political organisation for Chartists campaigning for the vote, Sunday schools for adults and children, and safe social areas for women who would not dream of going to a pub. In several places, such as at Clough Foot, on the road from Todmorden to Bacup, a Sunday School was built first in 1829, followed by a chapel in 1854 (see front cover).

Growth continued to rocket. As water-powered mills replaced hilltop cottagers' handlooms, the population moved down into the valleys and new chapels were needed. Some early buildings were soon bursting at the seams, some were knocked down and rebuilt, others split to form "daughter" chapels – or rivals.

In Todmorden, the modest Doghouse Lane chapel was replaced in 1827 with an enormous chapel and neighbouring Sunday School on York Street. Only 10 years later, the congregation acrimoniously split. The new society, in a shameless display of one-upmanship, built a "Methodist cathedral" only yards away, next to the Town Hall.

At Wainsgate, above Hebden Bridge, the first chapel built in 1750 had held only 100 people. It had been built so low that the congregation decided to dig it out by 18 inches, saving stone but making it extremely damp. When the legendary Dr John Fawcett became minister in 1764, his kind heart and generosity (he formed a circulating library from his own collection), as well as his gift for preaching, meant people came from miles to hear him.

His powerful preaching led to an invitation to become minister of a London chapel, which he accepted. The wagons were loaded but at the last minute he and his wife could not bear to leave their weeping friends and he remained in the area, remembering the incident in the ever-popular Baptist hymn "Blest be the ties that bind".

In 1777 he saw the growth in the valley and formed a new chapel in Hebden Bridge named Ebenezer, still in use as an art gallery. Wainsgate continued to grow, and was rebuilt in 1815 to hold 300 people, and again in 1860 to hold 700.

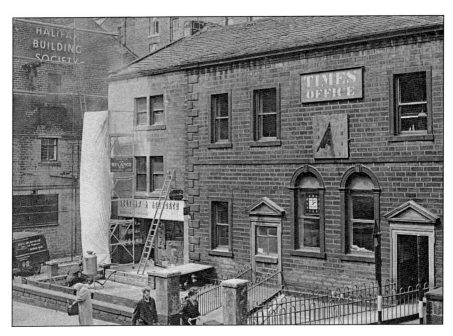

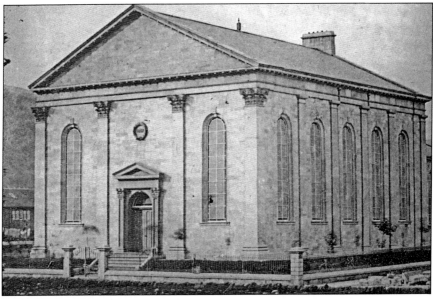

Top: the Ebenezer chapel, built in 1777, with a neighbouring manse, was replaced by the Hope chapel, above, in 1870 further along the road in Hebden Bridge. Since then Ebenezer has had many uses: as a Sunday School until the building which is now the town library was built, as the Hebden Bridge Times office and printers, as flats, an antique shop and now as the Heart arts centre with flats upstairs. Inside, the oddly irregular ceiling marks the original raked galleries. Hope chapel was under renovation at the time of writing but is still in use as a Baptist chapel with many groups using the back rooms, including a flamenco class and a burlesque class. Pictures courtesy of the Pennine Horizons Digital Archive.

The Slack Baptists' first chapel was the modest Robertshaws building (page 11). The congregation slowly declined but recovered thanks to the influence of Dan Taylor at Birchcliffe. The new chapel, top, was built in 1808 on the other side of the road, consisting at first only of the right-hand section with five regular upstairs windows. It was later extended with a manse added, then replaced with the present classical structure, above, in 1878. It was closed in 1973 and a group of wanted to buy it, causing local outrage amidst claims they had nailed a snake to the door. It was finally bought by an evangelical group who are slowly renovating it. Both pictures courtesy of the Jack Uttley collection, by kind permission of his son.

Broad-fronted chapels were usually re-ordered by the Victorians but these pictures of the modest Butts Green chapel at Luddenden, show a rare original arrangement with a pair of small pulpit windows to flank the preacher. This chapel is no longer in existence as the tiny remaining congregation decided they would rather have it demolished than turned into a house. Pictures courtesy Rodney Collinge.

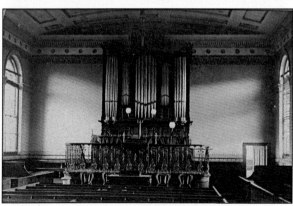

Interior and exterior of Luddenden Foot United Reformed Church. Built by millowners John and William Whitworth in 1859, it cost £5,500, roughly the equivalent of £3.7million today by average earnings. The lower part was a school for the mill workers, with a manse in one wing and vestries in the other. It is now flats. Pictures held at the West Yorkshire Archive Service.

By 1851, Britain's first religious census, held as part of the standard population census, showed that more people went to chapel than church. Clear dissident areas covered Wales, Scotland, Cornwall, the Yorkshire and Lincolnshire coasts, and a long strip stretching down the Pennines. The results caused the Establishment such horror and anguish that this was also the last religious census.

For the dissenters, it was proof positive that their brand of Christianity was destined to be Britain's dominant force. Confidence was sky-high. Not only were more chapels built, but they were bigger and grander than ever, in exuberant expectation that congregations would continue to grow exponentially. By 1880, 75 chapels had been built in the valley, and the movement was still growing.

How was this massive expansion paid for? These were generally churches of the working class, and in the 18th century were paid for by small donations, with tiny parcels of land often donated or bought and the people themselves labouring on the site. At Booth, in the Luddenden valley, the first Congregational Chapel was built in 1761 with no single member's donation being greater than a pound. The site, off Cow Lane, was almost inaccessible except to packhorses, and the men themselves dug the foundations, quarried the stone and formed a long line from the quarry to pass the stone by hand to the building site.

The placard reads "Young men in connection with the United Methodist Free Church, Luddenden, excavating foundation work, new chapel and school, May 1902." There was a long tradition of congregations assisting the skilled builders as labourers to bring down costs. The group has been perfectly posed but a handful of children at the back were determined not to miss the fun. Picture courtesy of Rodney Collinge.

But as the 19th century advanced, some of the working classes were doing better than they had in the days of hill farming and handloom weaving. Some had risen to become prominent millowners. Their confidence was high and their money was burning holes in their pockets. This often financially underpinned a new building, which had to be as magnificent as the sponsor's prestige demanded.

Two of the members of Booth Congregational Chapel were part of the Whitworth family, the chief employers at Luddendenfoot. They left the Booth chapel to sponsor the magnificent United Reformed Church on Halifax Road (picture previous page) which opened in 1859.

Ten years later the modest Booth chapel was itself replaced. Now built with generous contributions from Mr John Ambler of Peel House and Sir Titus Salt, it cost £4,000, far more than any other church in the Luddenden valley. Fronted with a huge rose window and topped with twin towers, it was described as a miniature cathedral which dominated the village.

Now was the battle of styles, with some embracing a free Gothic style with pointed windows and spires, and others choosing classical pillars and pediments.

One of the loveliest examples of Italianate classical architecture – and of the ever increasing ambition of the movement - is still to be seen in the Birchcliffe centre, Hebden Bridge, housed in the fourth and final chapel that sprung from Dan Taylor's ministry. At first he preached in a converted house, Higher Needless on the hillside near Old Town. The first purpose-built chapel, in 1763, cost £140, with Mr Taylor, a former miner, doing much of the work himself. In 1823 it was demolished and a new larger chapel built on the same site, costing £852. Overcrowded and suffering from dry rot, it was replaced further down the hillside. This final building opened in 1899 at a cost of £11,975 and is still open to visitors (picture page 77).

Below it is the Hope chapel, (picture page 16) replacing the Ebenezer chapel and also classically built. At the opening, the great-grandson of Dr Fawcett, Mr J.S. Wright said: "Your chapel is just what a Nonconformist chapel should be, not apeing the State-Church buildings by a spire costing as much as a mission room, or decorated after the style of an opera house."

He certainly wouldn't have approved of Todmorden Unitarian Church, now Grade 1 listed and lauded as one of the best examples of Victorian Gothic. It was built as a replacement to the original plain, but substantial Georgian chapel, which became a Sunday School and is now flats.

Architect John Gibson was given a free hand by the wealthy Fielden family and produced a soaring edifice that literally and figuratively overshadowed the parish church in the valley. No expense was spared on materials, from Devon marble to a stained glass rose window said to contain over 30,000 pieces. The interior is largely Anglican, the only dissenter touches are in the absences of crucifixes, or images of Mary or the saints. It is topped off with an octagonal spire and a full set of bells, operating like a giant musical box and programmed with six popular Victorian tunes, including Home Sweet Home.

Some parts of the Victorian establishment were furious at the presumption of the non-conformists in adopting ecclesiastical architecture to which

This interior of Todmorden Unitarian Church shows the Anglican layout, complete with altar, marble pillars and Gothic arched windows. The opening address was given by the noted Manchester Unitarian minister William Gaskell, husband of the novelist Elizabeth Gaskell. Part of his sermon argued that, despite Puritan doubts, there was nothing wrong in employing art to enhance religion provided this involved no compromise of inner sincerity. Picture courtesy of David Martin Photography, more of his pictures can be seen at http://dmartinhb.zenfolio.com. The church can be hired for conferences, weddings and other events.

they had "no right", as in this outraged editorial in "The Ecclesiologist" in 1847: "The Unitarians ..., horrible to tell, are building a meeting-house in florid Middle-Pointed. We heard that they intend to establish in it a kind of choral service, with vestments for their ministers."

Though perhaps they were also furious at their success in being able to pay for it. Supported by ever-wealthier mill-owners, the nonconformists forged ahead while the Anglicans must have been realising they had missed a trick.

In Heptonstall, the fabric of the old church (now a romantic and well-cared-for ruin) was neglected for a long time until part of the tower collapsed. The Anglicans, as the state church, applied for a church rate, an extra charge to be added to the local people's rates bills. But they received a public snub when the councillors, mostly non-conformist textile workers, would approve only a derisory farthing in the pound on the rates for the repairs. Stung into action, they raised a subscription to build a new church next to the old one, very firmly in the Victorian Gothic style and dominating

NEW WESLEYAN METHODIST
CHURCH AND SUNDAY SCHOOL,
FOSTER LANE, HEBDEN BRIDGE.

Stone Laying Services,
ON SATURDAY, AUGUST 20th, 1904.

PUBLIC MEETING IN SALEM CHAPEL.

KERSHAW & ASHWORTH, TYP., HEBDEN BRIDGE.

The distinctive Foster Lane chapel with its twin Russian domes was designed by local architect and lay preacher William Henry Cockcroft, who also designed the Blake Dean railway bridge and the Tin Tabernacle (see page 51). Stone laying ceremonies were widely advertised to pull in the crowds, with sermons sometimes being repeated during the day. Poster from the Jack Uttley collection, by kind permission of his son. Photograph of the ceremony, below, from the Pennine Heritage Digital Archive.

the surrounding cottages. Opened in 1854, it was clearly a matter of pride that it be larger and grander than any of the chapels springing up all around.

Pride must also have been operating amongst the non-conformists. Even where a major sponsor could not fund an entire building, the bar had been raised and chapels competed with bigger and better facilities. Even the tiny Hebden Bridge Dove Chapel, so-called because it met in a building formerly used for keeping doves, decided with only 18 members to raise funds for a new Zion Chapel with room for 250.

How did so many congregations do it? There was a well-used formula, with money being promised in advance and landmark events such as the stonelaying ceremony used as fundraisers. A prominent businessman or his female relations would be asked to lay the foundation stone, in expectation of a generous donation. Well-known preachers would be invited to pull in the crowds, with services throughout the day. A rainy stone-laying could cause a real financial difficulty.

Non-conformists were also unafraid to ask their congregations outright for cash, which was hastily counted at the back during services, as in the story of Old Town Chapel's anniversary services, recounted in the 1913 "Review of Methodism in Old Town".

"Amongst the men who preached the Anniversary Sermons during this early period the name of Richard Twemlow stands out prominent. He was a lay preacher from the Manchester district; a man of marked originality, and became quite a favourite with the Old Town people. He knew that good collections were essential, and his plea for 5 x s (meaning, of course, £50) is still remembered. On one occasion when the collections came a few pounds below the usual amount Twemlow buttonholed the officials, and heading the list himself with a handsome contribution, the desired total was obtained. Shortly afterwards it was discovered that one box containing nearly £5 had been overlooked in the counting.

"On one of his visits the Anniversary day turned out very wet; one of those warm growing days as they are termed, excellent for the springing grass, but decidedly unfavourable for new crinolines, hats and bonnets, and there was uneasiness lest the weather might interfere with the financial success of the undertaking.

"But Twemlow was equal to the occasion. At the close of one of his sermons he looked round on his congregation, among whom were a goodly sprinkling of farmers, and said "Now then, you farmers, it is raining sovereigns for you today; give the Lord His due; we want 5 x s." The appeal went home; the collection was a good one, and on the following day one old farmer made the declaration, 'Next time I goa to hearken owd Twemlow I'm taking nowt beside mi collection brass; he made me empty mi pocket yesterday.'"

Seat rents were another way of assuring a more regular income than collections at services. Only a few years after opening, Hope chapel interior, Hebden Bridge, had to be remodelled to provide more seating due to demand. As can be seen from the plans overleaf published in the 1897 Church Manual, people preferred, as now, not to sit in the front rows. Some churches took advantage of this, charging more for the back rows, as at Ludden-

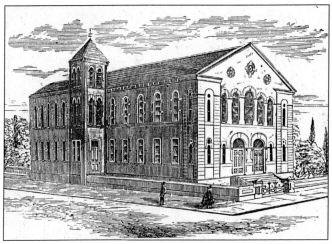

Top: Millwood, Halifax Road, Todmorden, was the descendent of the original Rod-well End building (see page 11). It had a gallery on three sides, supported by wooden pillars. In front of the tiny pulpit was a singers' pew which was also a communion pew. Below the end gallery was a vestry with a table"usually spread with a hand-some cloth; cupboards were constructed under the seats, containing various cooking utensils and crockery for the convenience of a few worshippers from a distance, who brought provisions for the Sunday dinner.... in the school hour it was used as a class room, whilst during services it was a convenient retiring room for mothers with their babies, who could listen and nurse at the same time... it was the deacons' vestry, class room, kitchen, tea room and the minister's sanctum."

When the congregation outgrew it, they built Roomfield chapel, above, in 1877. The chapel was continually short of money and it was demolished owing to dry rot, and replaced by a modern building. Millwood is still standing as a pet food suppliers. Though barely recognisable due to an extension across half the front, the word "Re-hoboth", meaning "The Lord hath made room for us", can still be seen across the lintel. Pictures courtesy of chapel historian Douglas Simpson.

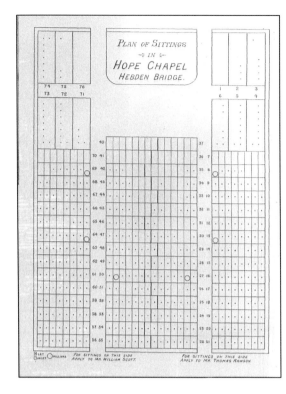

PLAN OF SITTINGS
→ IN ←
HOPE CHAPEL
HEBDEN BRIDGE.

This interior plan of Hope Chapel, taken from a Church Manual shows how even the fervent Victorians gravitated towards the back, reserved seats are shown with dots. The annual church manuals listed members' names and seat numbers, and gave accounts for the chapel, its Missionary Society, Sunday School and other groups. Visitors to Wainsgate are still greeted by a beautiful wooden pew board in a glass cabinet, with brass pegs to show reserved seats.

denfoot Methodist Church. Pew rents were 1 shilling a week at the front, graduating by 3d a time to 2 shillings at the back.

This practice of seat rents had drawbacks. The new, prosperous middle-classes could afford them but those still living hand-to-mouth could be left without a place. Though all chapels provided some free seats, these were sometimes not enough for demand, and may have left some poorer people, already embarrassed by their clothing, too ashamed to attend.

Even with all these sources of income, chapels such as Vale Baptist Church were still often built on credit, which had to be paid off by extra fundraising such as religious and social events.

East Riding historians David and Susan Neave wrote: "Although opponents accused the chapels of using teas, treats, entertainments, bazaars and the 'frequent introduction of female preachers and other exciting means' to increase membership, it was just such events that contributed to the vital role that chapels played in village life."

And what a life it was, full of friendship and controversy, music and education, entertainment of every sort, and above all, in a time of monotonous work, packed with incident.

Vale Baptist Chapel.

Grand ✴ Jubilee ✴ Bazaar,

THURSDAY, 31st OCTOBER, FRIDAY and SATURDAY, 1st and 2nd NOVEMBER, 1901.

OFFICIAL HANDBOOK.

Waddington and Sons,
Printers, &c.,
Fielden Square, Todmorden.

Never any stall I know,
Nicer things than ours can show,
Don't go by!

MARRIED LADIES' STALL.

FIRST DAY.

Mrs. STAINES,	Mrs. JOHN STANSFIELD,
„ JOHN SHACKLETON,	„ JAMES HELLIWELL,
„ ASHWORTH,	„ WM. SPENCER,

Mrs. DAWSON.

SECOND DAY.

Mrs. SAMUEL SUTCLIFFE,	Mrs. JOHN GREENWOOD,
„ JOHN HEAP,	„ W. SUNDERLAND,
„ B. ABBOTT,	„ G. H. HEAP,
„ WM. STONE,	„ FRED SOUTHWELL.

THIRD DAY.

Mrs. J. W. MITCHELL,	Mrs. WM. SHACKLETON,
„ A. MARSHALL,	„ THOMAS HELLIWELL,
„ SAMUEL FARRAR,	Miss SARAH GREENWOOD.

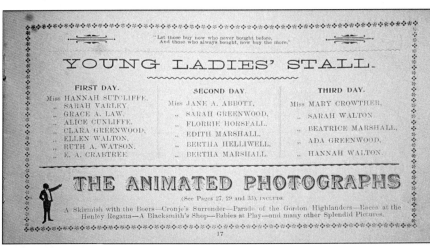

"Let those buy now who never bought before,
And those who always bought, now buy the more."

YOUNG LADIES' STALL.

FIRST DAY.	SECOND DAY.	THIRD DAY.
Miss HANNAH SUTCLIFFE,	Miss JANE A. ABBOTT,	Miss MARY CROWTHER,
„ SARAH VARLEY,	„ SARAH GREENWOOD,	„ SARAH WALTON,
„ GRACE A. LAW,	„ FLORRIE HORSFALL,	„ BEATRICE MARSHALL,
„ ALICE CUNLIFFE,	„ EDITH MARSHALL,	„ ADA GREENWOOD,
„ CLARA GREENWOOD,	„ BERTHA HELLIWELL,	„ HANNAH WALTON.
„ ELLEN WALTON,	„ BERTHA MARSHALL.	
„ RUTH A. WATSON,		
„ E. A. CRABTREE		

THE ANIMATED PHOTOGRAPHS

(See Pages 27, 29 and 33), INCLUDE

A Skirmish with the Boers—Cronje's Surrender—Parade of the Gordon Highlanders—Races at the Henley Regatta—A Blacksmith's Shop—Babies at Play—and many other Splendid Pictures.

17

Entertainments.

- - THURSDAY. - -

7-0 p.m.—OPERETTA, "Doll's Wedding," by the Children, in the School Room. Admission 3d.

7-45 p.m.—Baldwin's CINEMATOGRAPH EXHIBITION, in the Chapel. Admission 4d.

8-45 p.m.—PIERROTS, in the School Room. Admission 3d.

9-20 p.m.—Baldwin's CINEMATOGRAPH EXHIBITION, in the Chapel. Admission 4d.

SIDE SHOWS: Gramophone, Billiard Table, Shooting Gallery, Fish Pond, Sibbald's Models and Peep Show. (See programme on page 35).

This 36 page brochure for the Vale Baptist Church bazaar details the many stalls and attractions including the "Smallest Show on Earth" of tiny gold and silver models. These included a gold bicycle made of 102 pieces only one and three-quarters inches high, and a cherry stone containing a tea service, 21 spoons and two trays.

Married ladies were known by their husbands' first and last names, widows by their initials. Miss Sarah Greenwood seems to have joined their party, perhaps she was too old to continue on the "Young Ladies' Stall". Every possible way of raising funds has been thought of. The flower stall advertises: "It is expected that every gentleman will proceed to this stall and buy two buttonholes, one for himself and one for....". The refreshment stall, selling plain teas at sixpence and meat teas at a shilling, urges: "It is especially requested that Visitors will come to Tea, instead of after Tea, as ample provision will be made for their convenience." They cheekily add: "In connection with the Bazaar, a CLOAK ROOM will be provided. Although only the nimble PENNY is charged, the Generous are NOT prohibited from giving MORE."

Vale was an offshoot from Shore, originally meeting in the Pudsey Bobbin Works but later building their own chapel. The original outlay was £1,210, but, with typical ambition, they continued to expand, building a manse, Sunday School and larger chapel so never quite paid off the debt. This bazaar in 1901 finally cleared the last £450, but only a year later they drew up plans for a new school. As the congregation shrank in the 1900s, the main chapel was demolished and the Sunday School is now used instead.

Chapter Three
A cup of tea and a good sing

"The best things in life could be found within the church – good music, fine teachers, good literature and even the best wives."
Mr Priestley Crossley, of Mytholmroyd Methodist Chapel.

"The members of the senior classes intimate that they will prepare and serve a fruit tea – a sandwich tea – a picnic tea – a tea and meeting – followed by an interesting programme of entertainment consisting of recitations, sketches and glees – a lantern lecture – songs and choruses sustained by the Married Ladies and Gentlemen connected with the Chapel. Tea on the tables at 4.30pm."

So read dozens of posters, programmes and handbills, for every occasion imaginable: the opening of the new piano or the new crockery, the Sunday School anniversary, an Easter holiday, a New Year's Eve party, the reading of the annual accounts or a fundraiser for missionaries. Any reason or none was an excuse for a party.

And whatever the excuse might be, the meeting was really based around pickled onions and cakes. At Old Town, 350 regularly sat down for New Year, leaving memories "of snow-white table cloths, of gas brackets entwined with multi-coloured tissue paper, of strings of holly and paper roses looped from the ceiling, of seasonable mottoes decorating the walls, of the laughter of children, and the musical jingle of spoons and crockery, and there, amid pleasant surroundings, old friends met and exchanged greetings, and the prodigal came back – sometimes from a very far country indeed – and sat down once more on the old familiar benches."

The Mount Tabor ladies were justly famous for their teas, the menu always consisting of "home-made bread, cakes, buns, fatty cakes and pastries with cream in lavish quantities" charged at 6d for adults and 3d for children before the Great War.

These events both sprang from and created communities that had barely existed before. Methodist historian John Hargreaves said contemporary observers noticed the civilising effect chapel life had on what had been almost lawless areas. In 1766, William Grimshaw wrote that he was "venturing by divine assistance in a wild, unchristian place called Midgley", while Dan Taylor's biographers described the country as "remarkably wild and uncultivated; the inhabitants few, scattered and in general depraved".

As late as 1832 a man sold his wife in Midgley, while in Heptonstall the stocks were still in use in 1841 (they can still be seen near the car park). Cragg Vale was notorious for counterfeiting and coin-clipping on a scale so large it threatened to devalue the currency, while in Luddenden a cler-

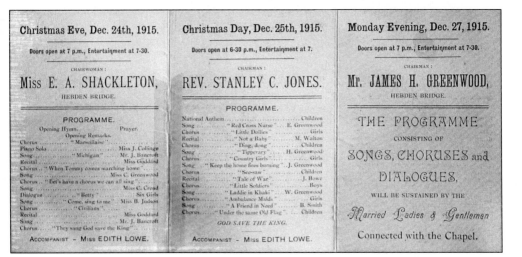

Christmas Eve, Dec. 24th, 1915.

Doors open at 7 p.m., Entertainment at 7-30.

CHAIRWOMAN:

Miss E. A. SHACKLETON,
HEBDEN BRIDGE.

PROGRAMME.

Opening Hymn. Prayer.
Opening Remarks.
Chorus .... "Marseillaise" ....
Piano Solo .... Miss J. Collinge
Song........................ "Michigan" ..... Mr. J. Bancroft
Recital .... Miss Goddard
Chorus .. "When Tommy comes marching home" ..
Song .... Miss C. Greenwood
Chorus .. "Let's have a chorus we can all sing" ..
Song .... Miss C. Croad
Dialogue .... "Betty" .... Six Girls
Song .... "Come, sing to me " .. Miss B. Judson
Chorus .... "Civilians" ..
Recital .... Miss Goddard
Song .... Mr. J. Bancroft
Chorus .. "They sang God save the King" ..

ACCOMPANIST - Miss EDITH LOWE.

Christmas Day, Dec. 25th, 1915.

Doors open at 6-30 p.m., Entertainment at 7.

CHAIRMAN:

REV. STANLEY C. JONES.

PROGRAMME.

National Anthem........................... Children
Song .... " Red Cross Nurse ".. E. Greenwood
Chorus .... "Little Dollies" .... Girls
Recital .... " Not a Baby " .... M. Walton
Chorus .... " Ding, dong " .... Children
Song .... "Tipperary".... H. Greenwood
Chorus .... "Country Girls" .... Girls
Song .... " Keep the home fires burning ".. J. Greenwood
Chorus .... "See-saw" .... Children
Recital .... " Tale of War" .... J. Howe
Chorus .... "Little Soldiers" .... Boys
Song............. " Laddie in Khaki " .. W. Greenwood
Chorus .... "Ambulance Maids " ...... Girls
Song .... "A Friend in Need " ...... B. Smith
Chorus...... " Under the same Old Flag " ... Children

GOD SAVE THE KING.

ACCOMPANIST - Miss EDITH LOWE.

Monday Evening, Dec. 27, 1915.

Doors open at 7 p.m., Entertainment at 7-30.

CHAIRMAN:

Mr. JAMES H. GREENWOOD,
HEBDEN BRIDGE.

THE PROGRAMME

CONSISTING OF

SONGS, CHORUSES and DIALOGUES,

WILL BE SUSTAINED BY THE

Married Ladies & Gentlemen

Connected with the Chapel.

Top: This three day "At Home" took place in the Heptonstall Chapel Sunday School, and has a markedly patriotic theme, reflecting the many members who would have been serving in the Great War. Kindly provided by Fay Fielding.

Right: The animated statutary seems to have had two parts: an animated slideshow of views, and a series of tableaux by members of the Sunday School. Another Hope Baptist Sunday School Sandwich Tea was organised by the young men, who were obviously determined to show what they could do. Their poster warned: "A fine of 1d will be levied on Ladies who assist or interfere in the management of above."

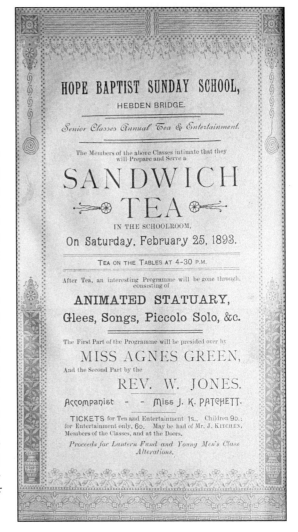

HOPE BAPTIST SUNDAY SCHOOL,
HEBDEN BRIDGE.

Senior Classes Annual Tea & Entertainment.

The Members of the above Classes intimate that they will Prepare and Serve a

SANDWICH
⇢❋ TEA ❋⇠

IN THE SCHOOLROOM,

On Saturday, February 25, 1893.

TEA ON THE TABLES AT 4-30 P.M.

After Tea, an interesting Programme will be gone through, consisting of

ANIMATED STATUARY,
Glees, Songs, Piccolo Solo, &c.

The First Part of the Programme will be presided over by

MISS AGNES GREEN,
And the Second Part by the

REV. W. JONES.

Accompanist - - Miss J. K. Patchett.

TICKETS for Tea and Entertainment 1s., Children 9d.; for Entertainment only, 6d. May be had of Mr. J. Kitches, Members of the Classes, and at the Doors.

Proceeds for Lantern Fund and Young Men's Class Alterations.

ic complained "the country people attributed everything of the marvellous kind to Robin Hood, as in Cornwall they do to King Arthur".

The non-conformists' organisation and emphasis on education wrought a remarkable change: in Blackshaw Head the Methodist chapel was actually built on the site of a bull-baiting ring.

In 1786, nearly 40 years after his first visit, Wesley visited Todmorden, writing: "How changed are both the place and the people since I saw them first! 'Lo, the smiling fields are glad; and the human savages are tame!'".

Whatever was wanted – sport, society, education, music – the chapel would provide, and for many it was all encompassing. Minutes from Luddendenfoot Methodist Church in 1868 show the members agreeing to move with the times and have two services on Sundays, instead of three. However, the next item discussed how members should instead spend Sunday af-

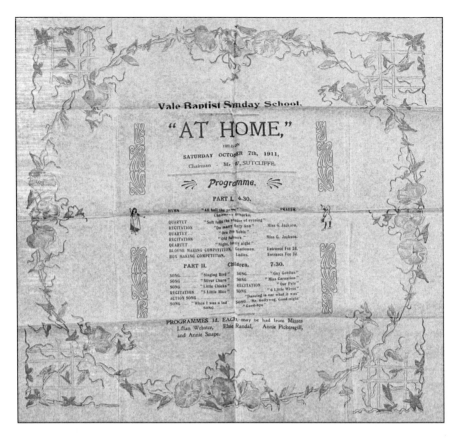

Above: This Vale Baptist "At Home" programme was printed on tissue paper, perhaps to be used as a napkin.
Left top: Members of Birchcliffe's sports clubs pose with bowling balls and racquets. Courtesy of the Pennine Heritage Digital Archive, source Philip and Sandra Lomas. Left bottom: these Pierrots and Pierrettes performed at Midgley chapel.Back: A Murgatroyd. L to r: J Holdsworth, Elizabeth Thomas, T Smith, L Crabtree, F Southwell, A Thomas. West Yorkshire Archive Service.

ternoons: it was decided to have cottage meetings between 2pm and 3.30pm.

Midgley Methodist Church was typically busy: it had not only the usual chapel and Sunday School with 42 teachers and 269 scholars, but also a Young People's Christian Endeavour Society, Look Out, prayer meetings, Social, Sick, Flower and other committees, a Chum's Hour for children and regular At Homes, concerts and social functions.

Men were reclaimed from the pub through PSAs, "Pleasant Sunday Afternoons", which seem to have been not much more than an excuse to sit and gossip without the women. Sports clubs were common: Birchcliffe had tennis, bowls and other clubs, while St James, Luddenden, had its own tennis courts and "many a marriage was made between the participants."

Education was for all ages, some chapels having extensive libraries. Sunday Schools taught more than literacy, and some chapels expressly sought to offer much more. At Vale, Todmorden, a "People's College" was opened in 1855, only four years after the chapel was founded, offering various subjects including History, Grammar, Physiology and Phrenology (a kind of psychology based on the size of the bumps of the skull).

The Young Men's Mutual Improvement Societies, later opened to ladies, acted almost as university seminars for the working class. At Old Town, the rules laid down that that each member should "exercise in all respects a courteous and gentlemanly demeanour". Sessions began with a member reading an essay of his own composition, which was then discussed. Titles included: "An Evening with Charles Dickens", "Comets and Meteors" and "The British People: Their Virtues and their Vices", with occasional less serious subjects such as "Colman's Mustard", which the records remark "was followed by a very warm discussion". Sometimes public lectures were arranged, and accumulated funds were usually spent on a waggonette outing.

Trips were common, from walks locally, particularly to Hardcastle Crags or Castle Carr at Whitsuntide, when the grounds were open and the fountains playing, to coach trips to the seaside. Some chapels even provided a kind of holiday through "camp meetings", relaxed two-day events of preaching and prayer with popular, rote-learned hymns as well as improvised and spontaneous music. Participants would meet at the chapel and walk up to the camp on the moor, singing as they went.

For some chapel was more than a place to worship or have fun – it was the place to see and be seen, so much so that there were occasional accusations of vanity. In Slack, a dressmaker heard an unkind rumour about herself that she only went to church to study the latest fashions, and ever afterwards kept her eyes closed in chapel. At Ebenezer, Hebden Bridge, one old man recalled a scandal of his childhood when Miss Bolton showed off her charms in a high-peaked gypsy hat, the latest vogue in 1811.

"In old Mary's eyes, anyone who could so conform to the world as to appear in God's house arrayed in such a head covering was far from being what she ought.... to the lady's surprise she pulled her bonnet down over her face, saying as she did so 'I like to see young Christians look modest!'."

But no fashion caused as much trouble as crinolines. Struggling over the stiles to chapel in a basket underskirt was a nightmare, and wet grass at a Sunday school picnic was destruction to them. Even worse was the issue at Shore, where the Sunday School committee despairingly reported: "It is dangerous to teach a class of girls around the stove because of the crinolines they wear."

Central to the life of the church, social and spiritual, was music. All over the valley, people loved "a good sing" and the chapels rang with praise.

The choir had a significant influence, and Victorian interiors often have a particular "singing pew" or gallery at the front with music stands. These choirs were taken very seriously: at Birchcliffe, when a singing school did not make the progress needed, the two leaders were pressed to go on, with the inducement of a shilling, a pint of ale and a penny cake each for every lesson.

Some choirs became nationally known: at Wainsgate, a musical society was formed in 1843 with the first secretary being Richard Ashworth. He

Top: A charabanc outing of Todmorden Unitarian Church Choir to Ingleton in the 1920s. The man sitting on the bonnet of the charabanc is Albion Barker, organist. Just behind him is the choir master, Harold Lees.

Bottom: Todmorden Unitarian Sunday School Queens. May Queens and Rose Queens were a common feature of summer parades. The girls seem to be enjoying the event more than the boys.

Both pictures courtesy of the Pennine Heritage Digital Archive.

Roomfield Baptist Choir photographed in the unusual setting of Foots Delph, below Beanhole Head, in about 1890. The choirmaster, standing at bottom right, is Charles Sutcliffe. Some of these ladies must have had a scramble in their hats and tiered skirts, but the end result, with carefully posed fans, is very elegant. Picture courtesy of the Roger Birch collection.

Top right: Luddenden accordion band was locally famous, playing at many processions including this Whit Walk of St James United Methodists. Picture courtesy of Rodney Collinge

Bottom: Slack Chapel Choir. Rev E.G. Thomas to the right of the conductor. Given by Esther Dean to the Pennine Heritage Digital Archive.

and his wife had nine children, five boys and four girls, all of whom joined the choir. The youngest, Alice, joined at 11 and remained an active member until her death aged 74 in 1943. In 1908, under Mr A.R. Ashworth, the choir won first prize at the Non-conformist Choir Festival at the Crystal Palace, London.

Initially, any music accompanied by instruments was seen as ungodly. John Wesley had spoken against the use of "mechanics" in music, and in 1808, the Yorkshire Conference of Baptists, meeting at Slack, declared the use of musical instruments in public worship to be "of human invention and totally improper". But the choirs in several places could see the benefits of accompaniment and began their own campaigns, sometimes starting with a single instrument which slowly built into entire orchestras. In 1840, Lineholme Baptist Chapel in Todmorden reluctantly noted:

"It was agreed for the sake of the peace of the Church to allow the singers to bring into the chapel and worship, another bass viol which they have, and to permit them occasionally to have one or two of their friends with other bass instruments. At the same time it was agreed by all, the singers pledging themselves to it, that no other instrument of music else than bass, at any time, or upon any occasion when the worship of God is conducted, be brought into this chapel."

At Slack, the choir was so determined to have instruments that they went on strike for several weeks, refusing to attend chapel, until the pastor wrote in friendly terms asking them to please "lay aside all idea of introducing instrumental music". They returned, but didn't give up the fight. After a long campaign, the daring innovation of a violoncello and a euphonium were introduced, with some members of the Church, strongly opposed, labelling them "Dagons", a half-human, half-fish god of the Philistines. One Sunday morning as the first hymn was announced, the euphonium player was about to blow the key-note when he discovered the mouthpiece had been unscrewed.

Years later, similar arguments attended the introduction of an organ. One "good brother of the old school", much hurt that his objections had been over-ridden, gave vent when he saw the organist and organ-blower walking up the path: "Stand back, the engineer and firer up are coming. They've spoiled me my sing and spoiled me my chapel. If I had my way, I would take out that new organ and tumble it down the Hebden."

The new fashion for organs caused problems in many places. An entire new sect, the Wesleyan Protestant Methodists, was formed in 1827 when a Leeds chapel opted to have an organ, in the teeth of opposition from their District Meeting. This had repercussions throughout the country, and prompted half the Mankinholes congregation, sick of the politics and in-fighting, to decamp to build a new chapel a couple of fields away. Ironically enough, 80-odd years later the chapel became home to a huge three-tonne organ still known as the Old Lady of Lumbutts.

Sunday School processions, Whit Walks and Band of Hope demonstrations were a common start to a day out with a picnic. The banners were often works of art. The one at the head of this procession on York Street, Todmorden, is Roomfield Baptist Church. From the Roger Birch collection, by kind permission of his son.

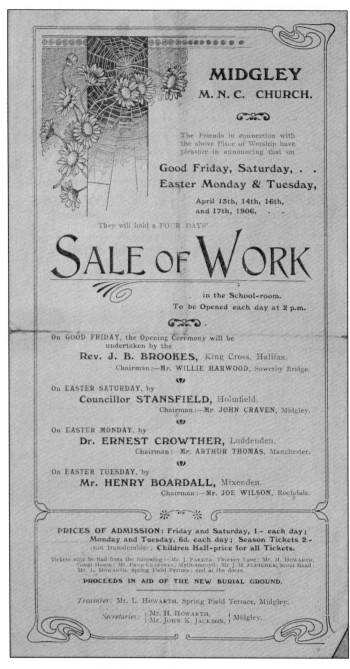

MIDGLEY
M. N. C. CHURCH.

The Friends in connection with
the above Place of Worship have
pleasure in announcing that on

**Good Friday, Saturday, . .
Easter Monday & Tuesday,**

April 13th, 14th, 16th,
and 17th, 1906, . .

They will hold a FOUR DAYS'

SALE OF WORK

in the School-room.
To be Opened each day at 2 p.m.

On GOOD FRIDAY, the Opening Ceremony will be
undertaken by the
Rev. J. B. BROOKES, King Cross, Halifax.
Chairman:—Mr. WILLIE HARWOOD, Sowerby Bridge.

On EASTER SATURDAY, by
Councillor STANSFIELD, Holmfield.
Chairman:—Mr JOHN CRAVEN, Midgley.

On EASTER MONDAY, by
Dr. ERNEST CROWTHER, Luddenden.
Chairman:—Mr. ARTHUR THOMAS, Manchester.

On EASTER TUESDAY, by
Mr. HENRY BOARDALL, Mixenden.
Chairman:—Mr. JOE WILSON, Rochdale.

PRICES OF ADMISSION: Friday and Saturday, 1/- each day;
Monday and Tuesday, 6d. each day; Season Tickets 2/-
(not transferable); Children Half-price for all Tickets.

Tickets may be had from the following:—Mr. J. PARKER, Thorney Lane; Mr. H. HOWARTH,
Great House; Mr. FRED CRABTREE, Mytholmroyd; Mr. J. H. FLETCHER, Scout Head;
Mr. L. HOWARTH, Spring Field Terrace; and at the doors.

PROCEEDS IN AID OF THE NEW BURIAL GROUND.

Treasurer: Mr. L. HOWARTH, Spring Field Terrace, Midgley.

Secretaries: { Mr. H. HOWARTH, } Midgley.
{ Mr. JOHN K. JACKSON, }

*"If you want an innocent, enjoyable Easter holiday, you could not do better than
pay us a visit!" says the reverse of this Sale of Work advert, which adds "There will
be a post office and snowball and various other things to amuse you. We should
like EVERY MAN to enter the Washing Competition and EVERY WOMAN to
watch", prizes supplied by the proprietors of Watson's Matchless Cleanser Soap.
The entertainments include a dialogue entitled "Woman's Rights" ("no woman
should miss it").*

Entire lives could be lived through the chapel, as seen in these photographs of Edith Stansfield, of Blenheim Street, Hebden Bridge, born 1913, who attended Hope Baptist Church with her parents Fred and Lillian. Below left, she appears in a pantomime and below right, a new dress for a chapel event demands a visit to Alice Longstaff's studio. White dresses like these were commonly worn for anniversaries.

In 1932, the frills were replaced with an elegant draped gown as she was photographed again by Alice, this time as Rose Queen, right. A family snap shows her atop the flower decorated wagon outside Hope Sunday School, now the library.

After the procession in Calder Holmes park, her neighbour Kenneth Crabtree asked if he could walk her home. They married at the church four years later and are pictured with bridesmaids Margaret Stansfield and Kathleen Shackleton and minister the Rev H J Blosse.

Pictures by kind permission of Edith's niece, Joan Baldwin.

Chapter Four
Sunday School

Inextricably linked with the chapel and all its events was the Sunday School. In the early days, free education was one of its great attractions, latterly, it formed the heart of the social calendar.

The Calder Valley was one of the first places in Britain to experiment with Sunday Schools, with the first recorded at Ebenezer Chapel, Hebden Bridge, in 1786. By 1833, there were 49 in the Upper Calder Valley, with 9,669 children and young people enrolled, 80 per cent of whom were non-conformists. Ten years later, the numbers had tripled. In some places, such as Clough Foot, near Todmorden, a Sunday School was built years before a chapel.

Even at the end of the century, when free education was almost universal, Sunday Schools were still very busy. In 1890, 38,000 Sunday School teachers and scholars descended on the Piece Hall, Halifax, for the last of the five-yearly "Whitsuntide Sings", commemorating the inauguration of the movement.

What made the Sunday Schools so enormously popular? The secret was the way they blended education and religion with entertainment, outings and prizes, in sharp contrast to most ordinary day schools.

After the Factory Acts of the 1830s and 40s made schooling compulsory for two or more hours a day, some factories ran their own schoolrooms and weren't minded to waste much money on them. At Lumb Mill, Colden, the schoolroom was 20ft long and 16ft wide. There were 51 pupils, 34 girls and 17 boys. The schoolmaster, John Marshall, was 23-years-old.

Writing in 1940, the Broadstones Chapel historian described how, in 1860 at Jack Bridge Mill, Colden, children from aged eight were up at 5.30am for work in the mill, eating breakfast there then working until 12.30pm. On alternate weeks they went to school from 9am to noon, home for dinner then worked from 1.30pm. Nonetheless, he described this as a bright period compared to the poverty of handloom weaving.

Large classes and cramped rooms meant discipline had to be strictly enforced, often through use of the cane or ruler. With few resources, little could be attempted beyond rote learning. The half-timers could be unwelcome even at full-time schools. From the teachers' point of view, dealing with them was frustrating. Though in theory they had to pass a final certificate before working full-time, in practice little was expected of them. Missing half of every day meant they were out of step with the work done by the rest of the class, they were exhausted by their mill work and sometimes fell asleep at their desks.

If life as a schoolchild was dull, it was little better for the staff. For teachers, as for children, it was probably better than being in the mill, but for

Top: The ornate ceilings of Heptonstall Sunday School are painted for the first time. Centre Jack Barker, right John Willie Whitham. Picture Eileen Longbottom.

Bottom: The Butterfly Queen pantomime at the Sunday School, 1914. Back: Winnie Greenwood, Tom Wrigley, Jimmy Smith, Mary Greenwood, Ethel Townsend, Gracie Greenwood, Fred Jackson, Harold Greenwood, Harry Shackleton. Middle: Marion Wilcock, Margaret Dixon, Ada Uttley, Irene Wadsworth, Marion Walton, Rhoda Smith, Dorothy Lowe, Nellie Sutcliffe, Emma Barker (Jack's daughter), Nellie Wild. Front: Ira Judson, Dilys Judson, Bertha Wilde, Helen Smith, Florence Sunderland. Picture courtesy Susan Marlor.

Miss Martha Bracken must have been proud to receive this splendid leather-bound, gilt-edged album from her girls at Booth Sunday School in 1874. It is filled with the carte-de-visite photographs of all her class, and is now kept at the West York-shire Archive Service.

the most part they must have been more occupied with crowd control than nurturing young minds. Women teachers were sometimes derided as old maids, as only single women could teach. Some led a lonely life, neither fitting in with their working class charges, nor having the status of married middle-class ladies.

Sunday School was very different. Being a Sunday School teacher gave a status in the community and a place at the heart of a buzzing chapel family. It was God's work, and volunteers gave their time out of piety.

There were enough teachers for fairly small classes. Typical enrolment figures (not all would attend on every Sunday) for Baptist Sunday Schools in 1890 are Hope, Hebden Bridge, (with Sowerby Bridge) 351 scholars and 44 teachers; Steep Lane, Sowerby, 280 scholars and 50 teachers; Roomfield, Todmorden, 423 scholars and 49 teachers. Broadstone Baptist Chapel recorded class sizes of between seven to 22 in 1845, from the first to fourth Alphabet classes, through the first and second reading classes, the first to third Testament classes and first to third Bible classes.

Attendance was voluntary (except for those children dragged along by their parents). Leaders knew they would win few souls by harsh treatment, so teaching was largely by kindness. The ultimate deterrent was temporary expulsion, though the sinner would always eventually be welcomed back into the fold. The 1812 "Rules for the Management of the Methodist Sunday School", published by a Midlands chapel, became a guide for many setting up Sunday Schools:

"The Teachers are expected to exercise much patience towards those who may be dull and stuped; to be particularly attentive to Servants and Apprentices, whose time of instruction is far advanced or uncertain, and who are very deficient in their reading; and also to such as are only in the rudiments...

"All, who engage in this Institution, are to give their labour freely, from a Principle of love to God, and a Regard to the best interests of the rising generation; without any pecunary reward whatever."

The Sowerby Congregational Church rules reminded scholars: "Ever remember that your teachers anxiously seek your welfare; make them, therefore, your friends; and by your cheerful disposition, loving confidence and prayerful spirit, endeavour to render their work pleasant, and to secure the blessing of God upon their labours."

This relationship could be so rewarding, it stood the test of time. The same church recorded: "A most pleasing ceremony was performed in the school room. Miss Rhoda Hanson having been a teacher in the Sunday School for forty-five years, it had been thought that her faithful and efficient services should be recognised in some tangible form. It was resolved that a portrait of her should be hung on the school wall, and on the above date it was unveiled ... The recipient suitably responded, expressing her appreciation of the honour done her, and her hope that God would spare her a little longer to go on in the work which was so dear to her."

For children, the Sunday School prize was part of the package from the offset. An Honour card or star card was marked for every attendance, one for each morning or afternoon session, with extra points for attending chapel services as well. The more points accumulated, the more costly the prize at the end of the year. These were always books, with inscribed book plates pasted into the front. Many were treasured possessions for years. In some chapels, such as at Heptonstall, the points were given as tokens to be exchanged at certain shops, so the recipients could choose their own books, possibly even exchanging them for a more expensive gift if a parent was willing to pay the difference.

Joseph Greenwood wrote about life at Ebenezer Wesleyan Methodist Chapel in Luddenden, where Sunday School was taught in the room beneath the chapel to children who may have walked miles to attend:

"On the boys' side, there were two long rows of hat pegs, where might be seen hanging an interesting batch of indescribable parcels... In those days, there was no heating apparatus as now; but there was a fire range in the corner of the Chapel bottom to the left of the preacher, and an iron stove in the aisle on the opposite side. It was in front of these where the Sunday mid-day meal was enjoyed so well, and where so often the possessor of a dainty bit generously gave to a less favoured brother or sister.

"The annual Tea and Meeting in connection with the School was a popular event. Tea was served on each side of the Chapel bottom, and inside the communion rails. At the meeting following, piano solos, recitations, songs and sketches were not then in vogue. There were speeches! speeches! speeches! And they were interesting ones too."

In most chapels, the children attended at least part of the service and many chapel minute books record the problems this caused – apparently children were as little used to being quiet and good during services as they are today. One exasperated Hope Chapel committee meeting stated:

"That we, as a Church, do not see the desirability of making any change in the arrangement of the Scholars' sittings in the Chapel. That we think the disorderliness of the scholars would be much lessened if the teachers would give a more regular and requisite supervision over them."

At Broadstone, Colden, they stood no such nonsense:

"Should a big boy attempt some breach of discipline, there was no escape. There was always some strong man ready to seize him when the service was over, and the penalty was to learn so many verses from the Bible before he went home. Sometimes a boy turned stupid, but it was no use, it had to be done."

Being a Sunday School scholar gave young people an entry into the life of the chapel, with all its social events and activities, even if their parents were not regular attenders. Many youngsters continued until marriage, leaving only to join the Mutual Improvement Societies. Chief of the special events were the Anniversaries and the Sunday School Treat, which were looked forward to for months - attendance always increased in the weeks before.

For Anniversaries, or "Charities", children would perform in front of the rest of the congregation, sometimes on a white-draped platform. Much like school concerts today, friends and relations would come for miles to see their little ones in the spotlight. In small rural chapels, they were often held outside due to the large numbers attending. At the tiny Crimsworth Dean chapel, near Pecket Well, the scholars sat in the yard to the side of

Top: Birchcliffe Sunday School "wedding", 1950s. Left to right, are: Geraldine Whipp, Anne Wilkinson (now Mrs Lomas), Penny Mitchell, Vivien Lord, Sheila Wrigley, Anne Greenwood (now Mrs Sutcliffe) and Lynne Greenwood (now Mrs Helliwell). Front is Elizabeth Snowball. Loaned by Miss Hazel Greenwood to Pennine Heritage Digital Archive.

Bottom: A performance by children of Hope Baptist Sunday School. Edith Stansfield is the second fairy from the left. Picture by kind permission of Joan Baldwin.

the chapel, with the choir on seats in Old Haworth Road in front (no problems with traffic in those days). Most of the congregation sat on the grass across the road and on the rising slope in front of the chapel. The Rev Johnny Gawthrope was a regular preacher for anniversaries, on one occasion he preached on the subject "Bless the lads, and the lasses will be Blessed".

Girls often had new clothes for Anniversaries. These were usually white, though at Midgley in 1820 one of the earliest church minutes is that "At all future Charity sermons none of the children shall be allowed to come dressed in white" – it was thought some were paying more attention to their clothes than to the sermon! This resolution seems to have been broken almost immediately. It was remarked in a history of Cross Ends chapel (the predecessor to Crimsworth Dean) that Susannah Ingham, a soloist for many years, had eleven dresses when she married in 1850, one she had got for each of the preceding eleven Anniversaries. At this chapel, there was a short-lived campaign to hold the Anniversary earlier in the year, so girls could start wearing their new summer dresses earlier after showing them off at the service.

The other big event of the year was the Sunday School outing or treat, often held at Whitsuntide, the seventh Sunday after Easter. In some places, these began with parades led by brass bands and choirs, though St James' United Methodist Church, Luddenden, boasted a 15-strong concertina band.

In villages, the Treat was usually an outing to the nearby field of a friendly farmer for games and a picnic provided by the church, though Old Town Methodist Church recorded one memorable occasion when waggons were provided for 130 people for a trip to Dyke Nook, near Oxenhope. The Ebenezer Wesleyan Methodist Chapel in Luddenden noted an outlay of 11 shillings and seven pence for bread, beer and cheese for the children in 1815, this continued to 1848. In those days, small beer was only mildly alcoholic and, because it had been brewed, was safer than drinking water. As the Temperance Movement gained hold later in the century, milk, coffee or tea was substituted, often with potted meat sandwiches, buttered buns and seedcake.

Historian Kenneth Young recorded how the great day often ended with the formation of "kissing rings", and the singing of old catches such as "The green leaves are falling", "Green grow the leaves on the old oak tree" "Oats and Beans and Barley" and "King William was King David's son", round games in which the odd person out chooses someone to kiss and swap places with. These days were the start of many romances.

In later years, with motor coaches available, treats became more ambitious. Susan Marlor remembers attending Sunday School outings from

Right: Sunday School libraries were a valuable resource before public libraries became common, and as much for entertainment as education. Hope Baptists (catalogue pictured right) had 1,860 books in 1897, including dozens of children's annuals such as "Chatterbox" and "Little Frolic". Plenty are aimed at girls as well as boys. Who wouldn't want to read Kate Marsden's "On Sledge and Horseback to Siberian Lepers", or Ed Bogg's "A Thousand Miles in Wharfedale"?

Sunday School treats and picnics were highlights of the year for poor families, as lyrically described in JL Carr's "Month in the Country", set in a Yorkshire village shortly after the Great War. The narrator has been hired to restore a wallpainting in an Anglican church, but is adopted by the local Methodists. After being recruited to help out with the Sunday School 'dafties', he is invited on the annual picnic:

There was a throaty smell blowing off the bilberry shrubs and the withering heather when we disembarked on a sheep-cropped plain high up in the hills. There was no shelter from the sun, but it was dinner-time and the women and girls unpacked hard-boiled eggs and soggy tomato sandwiches wrapped in greased paper and swaddled in napkins. It was Mr Dowthwaite (for you laboured for your prestige amongst the Wesleyans) who built a downbreeze fire of twigs and soon had tin kettles boiling. Then he struck up the Doxology and, when we'd sung it, we settled to some steady eating.

Afterwards, most of the men took off their jackets, exposing their braces and the tapes of their long woollen underpants, and astonished their children by larking around like great lads. The courting couples sidled off, the women sat around and talked. So, eating, drinking, dozing, making love, the day passed until evening came and the horses were led in from their pasture. Then, as the first star rose and swallows turned and twisted above the bracken, our wagons rumbled down from above the White Horse and across the Vale towards home: the Sunday School Treat was over.

8

NO.	AUTHOR.	TITLE.
1463	Craik, Mrs.	Olive
1496	,,	The Ogilvies
1497	,,	The Head of the Family
1464	,,	The Two Marriages
1860	Crockett S. R.	Bog, Myrtle and Peat
1861	,,	Clegg Kelly
1862	,,	The Grey Man
1896	,,	Lad's Love
1897	,,	Lochinvar
1760	,,	The Lilac Sunbonnet
1792	,,	The Men of the Moss Hags
1761	,,	The Raiders
1762	,,	The Stickit Minister
1793	,,	Sweetheart Travellers
1898	Dawson, W. J.	The Story of Hannah
1530	D. H.	The Greatest Thing in the World
1701	Davis, Ellen L.	Brook and River
1718	Davidson, Thain	Brave and True
1719	,,	Thoroughness
1575	Dilke, Sir Charles	Greater Britain
1539	Doyle, A. Conan	The Captain of the Polestar
1746	,,	The Firm of Girdlestone
1648	,,	Micah Clarke
1763	,,	Round the Red Lamp
1649	,,	The White Company
1899	,,	Uncle Bernac
1515	Edgar, John G.	Sea Kings and Naval Heroes
1879	Everett-Green, Evelyn	Arnold Inglehurst
1880	,,	The Young Pioneers
1650	Farrar Canon	Darkness and Dawn
1813	Fenn, G. Manville	Devon Boys
1900	,,	Frank and Saxon
1576	,,	Off to the Wilds
1577	,,	Syd Belton
1585	Fielding, Anne	The Stolen Shilling
1578	Fitzgerald, Percy	Three Weeks at Mopetown

9

NO.	AUTHOR.	TITLE.
1598	Fleming, James	Readings for Winter Gatherings
1599	,,	,, —2nd Series
1600	,,	,, —3rd Series
1540	Forbes, Archibald	Havelock
1715	Fothergill, Jessie	From Moor Isles
1833	Firth, Emma M.	Stories of Old Greece
1516	Franzos, K. E.	For the Right
1579	Frazer, Douglas	Perseverance Island
1882	Giberne, Agnes	The Girl at the Dower House
1651	,,	Will Foster
1720	Gillmore, Colonel P.	Travel, War, and Shipwreck
1901	Gaskell, Mrs.	North and South
1902	Gethen, H. F.	Nell's School Days
1903	Gould, S. Baring	Please Tell me a Tale
1680	Grace, W. G.	The Game of Cricket
1794	Graham, P. A.	Country Pastimes for Boys
1452	Gray, J. Comper Vol. I.	Biblical Museum
1453	,, Vol. II.	,,
1454	,, Vol. III.	,,
1455	,, Vol. IV.	,,
1456	,, Vol. V.	,,
1764	Gordon, W. J.	Everyday Life on the Congo
1652	Green, Hon. Mrs.	Gilbert's Shadow
1653	,,	The Schoolboy Baronet
1681	Greene, W. T.	The Birds in my Garden
1905	Grey, Maxwell	The Silence of Dean Maitland
1881	Greenhough, J. G.	The Cross in Modern Life
1784	Grimm	Fairy Tales
1863	Groves, Lieut. Col	Scotland for Ever
1517	Haggard, H. Rider	Allan Quatermain
1744	,,	Allan's Wife
1518	,,	Colonel Quaritch
1519	,,	King Solomon's Mines
203	,,	Maiwa's Revenge
1526	Hall, Salem & Mary E.	Seven Steps Upward
1541	Hamer Sarah Selina	Phyllis Raymond

Heptonstall, presided over by superintendent Sam Schofield, dressed in a suit, wing collar shirt, gold Albert chain and bowler hat:

"He stood there with a stick and you had to do as you were told. The first trip I can remember was to Townley Park in Burnley. Now it would be laughed at but it was an adventure to us. As time went on we started going to Blackpool and Southport.

"We had some hairy experiences. I remember on one trip one of the boys who was a bit boisterous frightened two girls in the Hall of Mirrors to death. Then on the way home the coach driver got lost and went up Mytholm Steeps and the same said boy was messing about on the back seat and put his bum through the window of the back seat of the coach.

"We also had a choir trip on Whit Monday if your parents sang in the choir. We went to Fleetwood or St Anne's and we were always booked somewhere to have tea, probably fish and chips but not as it is now, it was all china plates, china cups and saucers, lovely bread and butter. All the way home they sang hymns. We had some good times."

Heptonstall Wesleyan Sunday School form part of the Queen Victoria's Diamond Jubilee procession through the village, which has been decorated with Union Jack flags from several houses and an arch at the top of Towngate in the distance. Picture from the Eileen Longbottom collection.

Chapter Five
Sons of Poverty Assemble

See the brave, ye spirit-broken,
Who uphold your righteous cause:
Who against them hath not spoken?
They are, just as Jesus was,
Persecuted
By bad men and wicked laws.

Rouse them from their silken slumbers,
Trouble them amidst their pride;
Swell your ranks, augment your numbers,
Spread the Charter far and wide:
Truth is with us,
God himself is on our side.

"Sons of Poverty Assemble", Chartist hymn

Perhaps it's not surprising that the people who refused to worship the way the Government told them to should also have firm ideas about the rest of its pronouncements.

Unbowed by poverty and ignorance, the very formation of the chapels had been a political act. Those who can read, can organise: the Sunday schools were a weapon in the fight for fair wages, better working conditions, and, above all, the vote. Now able to read the Bible for themselves, they found plenty in it to support their cause. Their political and religious lives were inextricably linked.

As the 19th Century progressed, the non-conformists' hairsplitting over doctrine, which had led to so many splits and arguments, was gradually replaced with outward-looking social concerns. Their enormous energy and conviction of their own rightness was directed to action. Being largely working people, they were in favour of votes for all, or at least all men. The position regarding women was more complicated: some feared that if landowning women were given the vote, working people would be further outnumbered. Others felt true universal suffrage was too big an ask, and, of course, some were simply against it.

Many Chartist agitators were also lay preachers, bringing their politics directly into the pulpit in a way that foreshadowed South Africa's anti-apartheid campaigns. The combination of a training in public speaking, habits of self-determination and improved literacy inevitably produced activists. Ben Rushton was one of the most famous.

Born in 1785, he became a fancy worsted weaver in Ovenden and joined the Methodist New Connexion in Halifax. He was a Sunday School teacher and class leader, but became set against the concept of paid ministers and resigned from the Halifax chapel in 1821.

However, he remained a very popular lay preacher in the remoter areas of the Upper Calder Valley, tramping many miles every night to keep the spirit alive in struggling Chartist branches. Once a young colleague noted that Rushton's clogs were worn through to the sock. "Ay," said the old man, pausing only a moment, "but think of the reward hereafter."

He was invited to conduct the first Sunday School anniversary service at Luddenden Dean, and appeared in a clean brat (a voluminous woollen cloak), patched knee breeches, highly polished clogs and a tall hat.

He was a champion of the handloom weavers, who were on the brink of starvation due to years of falling prices, and preached with fiery eloquence of the poor "who had striven and worked hard all their lives, but had been made poor, or kept poor by the wrong doing and oppressions of others who had deprived them of their God-given rights".

By 1838, Chartism (the campaign for votes for all) was so well established in the valley that the Halifax magistrates applied to the Home Office for additional troops after reports of torchlit meetings on the Pennine moors, and Ben Rushton, already a seasoned campaigner (or "bald-headed old rascal" depending on your politics) was at the forefront.

Four years later, he was arrested during the "Plug Riots", so-called because the demonstrators pulled out the plugs of the factory boilers so they couldn't get up steam. More than 20,000 people, some with bare feet, marched through the valley to Halifax to demonstrate for the right to vote. Women made up the middle of the procession, and the Illustrated London News reported that some "hearty women" had walked from Oldham. They sang the hundredth psalm as they entered the town, and one of the campaigners' great banners read: "Be not ye afraid of them, remember the Lord, who is great and terrible, and fight for your brethren, your sons and your daughters, your wives and your houses". The Riot Act was read twice, and many, including Mr Rushton, were sent to York magistrates and so to prison.

Mr Rushton went on to speak at many mass meetings at Skircoat Moor, Halifax, and Blackstone Edge, at the top of Cragg Vale, where he once addressed 30,000 Chartists from Lancashire and Yorkshire from a rocky outcrop in an echo of John Wesley's outdoor preaching.

A Northern Star reporter commented: "There is something very attractive to the eye and to the ear of labour in this man's person and in his voice... his unswerving honour, his modest demeanour, indefatigable perseverance, have secured him the universal respect of his order."

Though he was at odds with some Methodist chapels by rejecting a paid ministry, his campaigning and his speeches were always based in his faith. He once preached at the opening of a Sunday School, housed in a Chartist reading room, a dirty garret in Foundry Street, Todmorden. Despite the surroundings, it offered a wider curriculum than most Sunday Schools, aiming to "render that instruction which will not only prepare the scholars to become good members of society, but give them the means of judging for themselves which party or sect is best fitted for their adhesion".

The "Plug Rioters" are pictured storming across North Bridge in Halifax on 15 August 1842 in the Illustrated London News. The six-span stone bridge was later replaced with the present iron bridge.

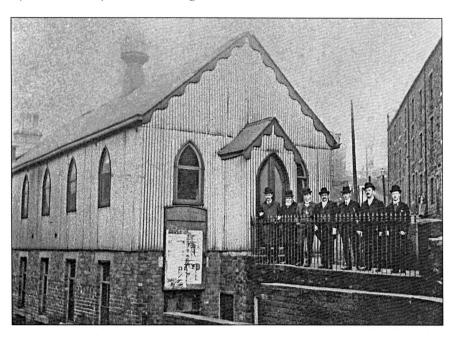

This modest "tin tabernacle" designed by local architect William Henry Cockcroft opened in 1887. A procession marched from here to the centre of Hebden Bridge to hear suffragette Mrs Pankhurst speak. These men may have been fustian workers, who made the chapel the strike headquarters in 1906. It was replaced by the grand Foster Lane building (see page 22) and was then used as a workshop. It became so dilapidated it was demolished in 2006 despite a local campaign to save it. Tin tabs, made of corrugated iron, were early pre-fabricated buildings. They were available for mail-order and were sent all over the empire. Picture from the Jack Uttley collection.

RULE XII.

Every person entering shall pay two shillings for entrance money, shall pay or cause to be paid one shilling per month afterwards, which shall be called the monthly contribution ; at every monthly meeting, each member shall pay off his contributions and fines, and in case of neglect, such member shall forfeit twopence a month for four months, such member to receive no benefit till the fifth contribution be called for, though he become sick or lame, until all contributions and fines be paid up, any neglecting the fifth time shall receive no benefit till the sixth, and if such member does not pay up the sixth time he shall be excluded.

RULE XIII.

When a free member is by hurt or sickness rendered incapable of working, he shall receive from the society's funds in weekly payments, after notice given to the visiting steward, the sum of ten shillings per week for the first eight weeks, and if he continue longer incapable of working, he shall then receive pay at the rate of five shillings per week for the next twelve weeks, and at the end of this time to receive three shillings per week during the remainder of his illness. Any member who has received full pay for eight weeks, and five shillings per week for twelve weeks, shall not be eligible to receive more than three shillings per week till he has been

clear of the funds for twelve months from the time of such sickness ; but should any member not have received the above amount, and fall sick again within twelve months he shall be allowed his full pay for the remainder of the eight weeks, or five shillings per week for the remainder of the twelve weeks, as the case may be.

RULE XIV.

No member shall be allowed to exercise any bodily labour, during the time he is receiving the benefit expressed in the last rule, and before they return to work, shall declare their recovery to the visiting steward, or forfeit sixpence ; and if the visiting steward, or any member, shall find that a member is working or using any bodily labour during the time they are receiving benefit from this society, shall be excluded if it is proved against them, to the satisfaction of the committee. Any member excluded for defrauding this society, shall not be re-admitted, except their accusation be found false.

RULE XV.

No member shall receive benefit from this society who is afflicted by the venereal disease, nor any who has received any hurt, or is become sick or lame from fighting, he or she being the aggressor, or drunkenness, and if on proof it shall appear to the committee that a member of this society has been intoxicated during the time he or she has been receiving benefit, or has been guilty of any

irregularity tending to lengthen or increase his or her disorder, shall forfeit ten shillings or be excluded, as the committee shall think proper.

RULE XVI.

When any member, residing within three miles of Sowerby Congregational School, becomes sick or lame, and requires benefit, he or she shall send his or her case to the visiting steward. Any indisposed member residing beyond the distance of three miles, must send a letter, post paid, to the president, treasurer, or one of the stewards, signed by a doctor, and a similar letter must be transmitted every fourteen days during such indisposition, and the weekly benefit will be sent to his or her order; and when such indisposed member becomes able to work, shall send a letter in like manner, signifying his or her recovery.

RULE XVII.

No female member of this society shall be allowed to receive any benefit during her pregnancy, except she have the misfortune to break a limb, or happen some other providential accident, provided she should have received any thing during forty weeks of her delivery, she shall refund it or be excluded ; but on the birth of a child borne in lawful matrimony, shall receive five shillings for the first month, if she have paid to the society one year; and if she should continue

indisposed, she shall be entitled to the same relief as any other such female member, but she shall not be entitled to any thing on a premature birth.

RULE XVIII.

On the decease of a free member, the sum of six pounds shall be paid by the treasurer, as soon as demanded by his widow, executor, or administrator, or any person duly authorized to receive the same on behalf of the deceased, first deducting all arrears and fines from him due to the society at the time of his death. The two visitors, for the time being, shall attend the funeral free of expence; also half-members shall receive money in proportion.

RULE XIX.

If a member be convicted of felony, or embezzlement of money, in the discharge of any of the offices of this society, he or she shall be for ever excluded

RULE XX.

If a member shall conceal any fine incurred by another member for breach of these rules, or any offence committed in violation of them, he or she shall pay the same fine as the person offending.

Sowerby Congregational's society admitted females, but only as "half a member", and there were no pay-outs for complications due to pregnancy. In fact, any condition that was considered to be self-inflicted was excluded from payout, as rule XV shows. By kind permission of John Kerridge.

He died aged 68, in poverty and without medical attention, after suffering from jaundice for several months. The Chartist executive decreed a public funeral (without any paid ministers officiating), and his coffin was accompanied by a brass band and a marching column of Chartists that took an hour and a half to pass, on a route lined with people. At least 6,000 people attended, and Karl Marx reported it in his bulletin in the New York Daily Tribune.

Nor did chapels just produce activists, they were also powerful co-operatives, acting to protect their members from hardship. Though bank accounts were still a rarity for all but the most wealthy, chapels formed their own institutions. A people who, only a generation earlier, had been illiterate cottagers were now running regulated financial schemes, managed by committee.

The Benevolent Societies were formed as early insurance services, paying out when members were too sick to work, even providing some maternity cover, at least for legitimate pregnancies (see left).

Funeral societies were formed to enable the poor to pay for their funerals. One at Hope Chapel, Hebden Bridge, was expressly for Sunday School teachers and scholars, so that parents could meet the expenses of burying their children. Payments by members were discontinued whenever there was a certain amount in the kitty, until payouts lowered the fund again. After many years it hit an unexpected snag: "The exceptionally healthy lives of the members, though satisfactory in one sense, must to a certain point increase the financial risk of the Society, since it is raising the average age of the members." The committee finally decided to begin investing the money, while altering the rules for new members.

Church officials also acted as judge and jury in some cases, disciplining members by public humiliation. Slack Baptist chapel records include cases of illicit drink-selling, gambling and of "a person charged with breaking a man's leg while playing football on Sunday; that of a woman accused of throwing a log of wood at the head of another; and that of a man who led his blind son to public-houses, and left him there to fiddle for drunken persons."

By the late 19th century, one of the defining organisations of non-conforminst life was formed, the "Band of Hope" or Temperance movement, founded in Leeds in 1847 and aimed at reducing alcoholism by teaching children "the evils of drink". It wasn't welcomed everywhere – in Sowerby two chapels banned all temperance meetings, resulting in a new Providence United chapel being formed in 1875.

The Band of Hope provided children's clubs, with activities, magic lantern slide-shows, parades, the crowning of rose queens and all the usual Victorian amusements. Band of Hope parades were common in the valley. Each group would march from their own chapels behind their own embroidered banners, meeting up in town centres for grand demonstrations. Some meetings drew crowds of many thousands, with bands and other entertainments.

Children were encouraged to "sign the pledge" to abstain from intoxicating liquor. The movement also funded research into the effects of drink, pro-

" Her home, dark and degraded by her husband's drunkenness."—p. 43.

The Band of Hope produced a children's magazine "Onward". This image, from a story "Let it alone" featured in 1882. The magazine often included images of the effects of drunkenness that would be considered unsuitable for children today. It was believed children would act as missionaries in the home for the temperance movement. Some stories show adults being shamed by their children, such as "Bessie's Bun", where a child is reduced to begging because her drunkard father has wasted his wages in the pub. This image is held at the University of Central Lancashire's Livesey Collection.

ducing early observations of the low-birthweight of babies born to mothers who drank heavily. Queen Victoria became patron in 1897.

Unfortunately, its joy-killing, wet-blanket associations probably did more than anything else to define the non-conformists as worthy-but-dull right through the 20th century – a far cry from their firebrand roots.

Children and adults who signed the pledge were awarded certificates to remind them of their promise. This one belonged to Florence Hesselden of Midgley Methodist Chapel, and is now held in the West Yorkshire Archive Service.

Chapter Six
A Homely Spirituality

Parties and politics may have formed the fun and flavour of chapel life, but its beating heart was a Christian spirituality born and bred of the North.

For baptists, the defining moment of entry into the body of Christ was the ritual of baptism, a total immersion in the running waters of their homeland which washed away all sins and gifted them the keys to heaven. In the early days, a nearby stream would be dammed a few days before the ceremony, and the hollow allowed to fill to provide a baptismal pool. The congregation, sometimes of several hundred people, would gather on the hillside to witness the ceremony, followed by services lasting all day back at the chapel. At Slack, female candidates were provided with dresses made from "shalloon," a lightweight but tightly woven wool fabric. There was no concession to the weather. At Shore in 1850, one baptism was held on Christmas Day. A Birchcliffe historian wrote:

"Fervent were they in those days! Good old soldiers of Christ! One candidate being so desirous of joining the happy band of Jehovah's followers, that though seeing the river in which she should be immersed frozen over, she bravely broke the ice around her, and thus entered the fold."

In later years, baptistries were built into chapels, or sometimes immediately outside them, which at least saved the long walk back up the hill in a wet woollen dress. Millwood in Todmorden had one fed by a spring under the floor.

This picture opposite appeared in a children's picture book in 1896. The text read: "This rather strange scene represents a ceremony of the Baptist body, according to whose special tenets the rite of baptism can only be administered to persons who are " converted " and are believers in the doctrines of the Christian faith, and not to infants. In this instance the minister, with the person to be baptised, steps down into a little open-air baptistry, and each candidate in succession is fully immersed. The most inclement season of the year is no obstacle to the performance of this religious duty; and on a very recent occasion it is recorded that five young men and one young woman were immersed in an out-door baptistry in Yorkshire in the month of February, when much snow had to be cleared away in order to approach the water."

Note the poorer women with shawls over their heads in contrast to the fancy hats of the better off. The minister has his hand on the back of the baptism candidate to support her; she will lean on him as he dips her backwards underneath the water three times.

Once a part of the congregation, everyone was encouraged to speak up with shouts of "Amen" and "Hallelujah" in a way unheard of in the formal established churches. One feature was the "Love Feasts", where the congregation passed around a two-handled cup of water and baskets of bread

THE BAPTISM OF A BELIEVER: A SCENE ON A YORKSHIRE HILLSIDE.

Broadstones: This was the second Broadstones chapel, near Colden, and was described as a place of "sweetness and light". The first chapel was so small that when the preacher stood in the pulpit, his head and shoulders could be seen only by those in the gallery, and the rest of him by the people below. Picture from the Jack Uttley collection, by kind permission of his son.

(though at Mytholmroyd they had ratafia biscuits) while taking turns to testify and pray.

Joseph Greenwood's "Reminiscences of Luddenden Methodism" said that in 1840: "one of the things looked for when the new plan arrived (a calendar of church events) was the date of the next Lovefeast.... One after another the listeners rose and related the marvellous dealings of God with them! It was grand to listen to their heartfelt testimonies. They made us smile through our tears of joy and sympathy. Their descriptions of God's dealings with them were so pointed and pithy that it was good to be there."

Freed from the strictures of the liturgy, chapel members could create their own prayers which, though not always reaching the unparalled beauty of the Book of Common Prayer, were nonetheless heartfelt. Pastor E G Thomas recalled one old man who often said "We thank Thee, O Lord, that in heaven we shall have crowns that need no fettling."

Smaller prayer meetings were a regular feature of non-conformist life, sometimes called "experience meetings" by Baptists, because members related their recent experiences,or "class meetings" by Methodists. These had nothing to do with social class, but were simply small groups of church members who met together with their class leader for Bible study, discussion and prayer. Members might tell of their difficulties, failings or triumphs. These could create a deeply spiritual experience, as The Historical Review of Broadstones, Colden, which may have been written by John Sutcliffe of Shaw Lane, evocatively records, writing of the late 19th Century:

"One took place in Laneside. This is a Farm at the roadside, next to the moorland road leading to Egypt, Reaps and Gorple. No one would think in those days of two reservoirs in that valley. In winter-time on frosty nights, sometimes with a full moon, it was a treat to walk along the road, and when you got inside there was a fire built from peat right up into the chimney. The living-room was large, and we had benches to sit on. Three men lived there – no woman, and the house was clean, the floor scrubbed and sanded. To light the room there was nothing but candles, which were hung on strings at intervals, and during singing Mr Stansfield went round snuffing these candles.

"Meetings were also held at Shackleton Hill, the home of Mr Paul Thomas, and no-one who had the privilege of going there will ever forget it. First the walk through the woods by Hardcastle Crags and through narrow lanes to the Farm. On entering you met Mr Thomas himself, who bade you welcome in his hearty fashion. Standing there to receive you – he must have been more than six feet in height, and broad in proportion – clad in his breeches and leggings and heavily nailed boots he made you imagine Oliver Cromwell would be something like him. Standing up he reached almost to what was called the "Bread Creel" a place where Oatcake was dried. When he knelt down by the benches, and his voice thundered out "let's have a word of prayer," one could never forget the feeling as he spoke, and when the old Grandfather Clock in the corner whirred out the hours the picture was complete."

The basis of non-conformism was teaching, not ritual, with the pulpit being given central place in chapels and meeting houses.

In the early days, preachers set out to provide hours of education, exhortation and entertainment – the length of sermons slowly reduced but many preachers would count through the sections with "firstly", "secondly", "thirdly" and so on until they eventually reached "Finally...", doubtless to the relief of listening children, and possibly some adults.

In theory anyone could have a go, though in practice almost all preachers at mixed gatherings were men until the 20th century. Though larger chapels employed paid ministers, lay preachers, who might be farmers or weavers during the week, often took to the pulpit. Smaller chapels in out-of-the-way places, such as Blake Dean at the top of Hardcastle Crags, had no paid ministers at all. Some preachers were doubtless better than others, but hearing from your contemporaries rather than just your "betters" was part of the democracy of non-conformist life.

The opportunity to learn public speaking was also a valued one, which doubtless prepared many young people for local political life. The Baptist Times, which was published in many editions and contained several pages of local news, often encouragingly mentioned the first efforts at preaching by young men.

The Broadstone Chapel historian remembers some preachers' idiosyncracies:

Blake Dean, at the top of Hardcastle Crags, never had its own minister. It was built in to the hillside by a couple of hairpin bends, with doors at the top level as well as the bottom. Worshippers walked down a short flight of steps to the galley entrance and up a flight to the main entrance, leading to the phrase: "downstairs to the gallery and upstairs to the bottom". Now sadly demolished. Picture from the Jack Uttley collection, by kind permission of his son.

"There were some peculiar characters. Mr William Hollinrake came with top hat, much the worse for wear, a black suit, the coat cut away at the bottom, and bright buttons. The look on his face, with its large overhanging eyebrows, was something which impressed you very much. When he engaged in prayer at the close of service, his final words invariably were, 'Have nothing to do but retire, undress and sleep in Christ and righteousness.'...

"John Uttley, a farmer, of Heptonstall, was a very earnest preacher with a method all his own. Wherever he took his text he brought in the journeyings of the Children of Israel, and one always knew that this would come in. His holding of his manuscript down with the left hand whilst beating the air with his right was well remembered."

A respectful account of the life of James Hodgson, of Stubbing House, Hebden Bridge, nevertheless concludes: "It is said his sermons were invariably long. We are told that they were also dry, though of a solid kind; and for this reason, boys and girls were exceedingly reluctant to attend chapel, whenever they found Mr Hodgson planned to preach; some could only be induced to go by having a good supply of sweet parkin to take with them." When he preached at Slack, some boys used to slip away and "borrow" his horse for a ride on Popples common.

Tent revival meeting, Beaumont Street, Todmorden, 1900s. Travelling preachers exhorted sinners to come and be saved. Some were charismatic, with a strong feel for showmanship. Contemporary observers claimed they created a kind of hypnosis. In her book "Oranges are not the only fruit", Jeanette Winterson described how her adoptive parents were "saved" at a revival meeting. Picture from the Roger Birch collection, by kind permission of his son.

Some Methodist preachers were so enthusiastic, they became known as Ranters. Todmorden historians Dorothy Hargreaves and Linda Briggs wrote of Knowlwood Chapel (pictured overleaf): "Not long after the original chapel opened its doors, a preacher by the name of Mr. Hutchins from Pexwood in Todmorden arrived...

"He often worked himself up into a frenzy of excitement, and on many occasions he would discard his coat, place it on the edge of the pulpit from where it would fall into the orchestra, and then he would walk down the steps gesticulating in a vehement manner declaring he could see the devil, calling out "I see him, I see him! Can you see him?" Many of his congregation would fall into a trance and purport to have seen God and Heaven. Fortunately, his preaching worked on some of the people, who became more sober in their habits.

"Mr Hutchins had a young nephew living with him by the name of Joel Hodgson. At the age of about 14 he was put in the pulpit. His enthusiasm caused havoc amongst the congregation. His fire and brimstone style was too much for the older ladies, who withdrew their support until a more rational preacher could be found, and one who was a little older than 14. The uncle and nephew were the talk of the neighbourhood during the year 1837 because of their use of strong language and outrageous gesticulation. So much so, that many people attended the Sunday evening services to see for themselves."

The fire and brimstone style of some ranters inevitably lent itself to satire. Stella Gibbons brilliantly captures the entertainment-value to be had from a good preacher in Cold Comfort Farm, in which Londoner Flora Poste is forced by lack of funds to live with her passionate and chaotic rural cousins. Here, she is obliged to listen to her cousin Amos's sermon in the tiny chapel of the fictitious "Quiverers":

Knowlwood.
The Primitive Methodists were generally drawn from the poorest classes, and this substantial Italianate chapel and school represented a great undertaking for them.
It was demolished and replaced with a bungalow.

The texts on the wall read "Seek ye the Lord while He may be found", "Children obey your parents", "Christ and the Church", "Wine is a mocker", "Blessed are the peacemakers" and "Put on the whole armour of God". In the roundels above, Praise has been added to the usual Hope, Faith and Love. Both pictures from the Roger Birch collection, by kind permission of his son.

For some three minutes he slowly surveyed the Brethren, his face wearing an expression of the most profound loathing and contempt, mingled with a divine sorrow and pity. He did it quite well. Her heart warmed to Amos. The man was an artist.

At last he spoke. His voice jarred the silence like a broken bell.

'Ye miserable, crawling worms, are ye here again, then? Have ye come like Nimshi, son of Rehobam, secretly out of yer doomed houses to hear what's comin' to ye? Have ye come, old and young, sick and well, matrons and virgins (if there is any virgins among ye, which is not likely, the world bein' in the wicked state it is), old men and young lads, to hear me tellin' o' the great crimson lickin' flames of hell fire?'

A long and effective pause. The only sound (and it, with the accompanying smell, was quite enough) was the wickering hissing of the gas flares which lit the hall and cast sharp shadows from their noses across the faces of the Brethren.

Amos went on: 'Aye, ye've come.' He laughed shortly and contemptuously. 'Dozens of ye. Hundreds of ye. Like rats to a granary. Like field-mice when there's harvest home. And what good will it do ye?'

Second pause.

'Nowt. Not the flicker of a whisper of a bit o' good.'

He paused and drew a long breath, then suddenly leaped from his seat and thundered at the top of his voice:

'Ye're all damned!'

An expression of lively interest and satisfaction passed over the faces of the Brethren, and there was a general rearranging of arms and legs, as though they wanted to sit as comfortably as possible while listening to the bad news.

'Damned,' he repeated, his voice sinking to a thrilling and effective whisper. 'Oh, do ye ever stop to think what that word means, when ye use it every day, so lightly, o' yer wicked lives? No. Ye doan't. Ye never stop to think what anything means, do ye? Well, I'll tell ye. It means endless horrifyin' torment, with yer poor sinful bodies stretched out on hot gridirons in the nethermost fiery pit of hell, and demons mockin' ye while they waves cooling jellies in front of ye, and binds ye down tighter on yer dreadful bed. Aye an' the air'll be full of the stench of burnt flesh and the screams of your nearest and dearest...'

He took a gulp of water, which Flora thought he more than deserved. She was beginning to feel that she could do with a glass of water herself.

Amos's voice now took on a deceptively mild and conversational note. His protruding eyes ranged slowly over his audience.

'Ye know, doan't ye, what it feels like when ye burn yer hand in takin' a cake out of the oven or wi' a match when ye're lightin' one of they godless cigarettes? Aye. It stings wi' a fearful pain, doan't it? And ye run away to clap a bit o' butter on it to take the pain away. Ah, but' (an impressive pause) 'there'll be no butter in hell!'

Chapter Seven
Women Find a Voice

Without a doubt, the non-conformist movement has benefited women and been a driving force for equality in many ways. The Sunday School movement probably benefited girls more than boys, for where little money was available for education, it would almost certainly be spent on sons not daughters, as is commonly the case in the Third World today. There was no financial barrier to entry at Sunday Schools, where the ability to read God's word was to be made freely available to all.

For adult women, Mutual Improvement Societies and evening classes opened up the world far beyond narrow rural or provincial life. Entertainments and At Homes gave a chance for creativity and self-expression in a safe and respectable environment at a time when "actress" was a synonym for "whore".

And although the Temperance Movement may seem moralistic today, in a time when drink-fuelled domestic violence was common, many women may have been glad when their husbands signed the pledge. One of its most famous campaign posters showed a lovely young woman under the slogan "Lips that touch liquor will never touch mine". The Art Nouveau scrolls are quaint by today's standards, but perhaps she was as much a standard-bearer for mastery of one's own fate as Rosie the Riveter.

There's no need to look further than the state of most churches today to know that women have played a major part in the life of the non-conformist movement. Alas, then, that their voices are so under-represented in the records.

This is made all too clear in remarks such as this in one of the official histories of the Birchcliffe Chapel: "In 1763, Dan Taylor started preaching to a congregation of four people who had gathered under a tree at Nook, in Wadsworth. No record has been kept of the name of a woman in that first congregation, but the other three were John Slater, John Parker and William Crossley."

In his poem on the centenary of Heptonstall chapel, the author spends 15 verses naming its renowned preachers and ministers before finally adding:

"Some right holy women have worship'd God here,
Their spirits were meek, ornamented with fear;
Like Mary of old, they had chose the good part,
And nourish'd the deep hidden man of the heart."

Until the 20th century, few, if any, women held office in chapel life, except in the Sunday Schools. Some chapel histories boast of their working class

Above: Yorkshire Baptist Association Meeting helpers, who organised a major conference in Hebden Bridge in 1911, pictured here in front of the Hope chapel manse. The notes on the back say: "Ada M C in doorway of Manse. On Ada Marianne Crossley's right, daughter Phyllis Crossley, on her left elder daughter Muriel Crossley – on <u>her</u> left, Mrs Owen, wife of then minister."

Right: Plans by the organisers. The menu was: beef, mutton, white and brown loaves, dinner buns, salad of tomatoes, cucumbers, lettuce and parsley (three pence worth would have been enough!), stewed prunes, figs and rhubarb, fruit tarts and custards, sultana cake, mixed tea cakes, mixed buns, eccles cakes and turnovers, cracknels (a type of hard plain biscuit) coffee and cheese biscuits. Picture and plans held at the West Yorkshire Archive Service.

The first day. Tuesday. the friends came for lunch more than half an hour before the appointed time owing to the shortness of the service in the Chapel. In spite of this we were quite ready for them. + within 5 minutes of the tables being filled - every person was served with meat.

Numbers for lunch + tea.

	Tuesday	Wednesday
Lunch	360	275
Tea	450	350

There were 400 luncheon - + 600 tea tickets printed.

roots, with lists of trustees including labourers, yeomen, and spinners, but women's names are very scarce indeed. I have found no women trustees, though they do occasionally appear as founding members. Susy Sheard was listed last behind ten men as the only female founding member of the Zion Strict and Particular Baptist Chapel, Hebden Bridge, in 1839; and at Brearley, the listed founders were eight men and women, all from three families, originally from Hebden Bridge's Ebenezer chapel.

Neither Baptists nor Methodists allowed women to be ministers (a formal paid post which includes administering Holy Communion) until the 20th century. John Wesley allowed a small number of exceptional women to preach to mixed groups in public, but this was all but banned after his death.

Some breakaway Methodist groups, including the Primitive Methodists, allowed women preachers, but they remained rare, except at women-only gatherings. Perhaps the women themselves were reluctant to expose themselves to criticism or even ridicule: Samuel Johnson's jibe about women preachers had been much repeated. (Boswell's Life of Johnson recorded: "I told him I had been that morning at a meeting of the people called Quakers, where I had heard a woman preach. Johnson: "Sir, a woman's preaching is like a dog's walking on his hind legs. It is not done well; but you are surprised to find it done at all.")

The Baptists rather grudgingly handed over some authority: in 1719 the Yorkshire Association decided women were permitted to vote in church meetings – unless there were more women than men present.

In terms of officials, Roomfield Baptist Church, Todmorden, provides a typical snapshot. All officers were male from its first beginnings in 1704 at Rodwell End, throughout two centuries. In 1923, a resolution was passed "that in future, females as well as males be eligible for membership of the diaconate and that the elections be by ballot." But church historian Douglas Simpson says that despite this, retiring male deacons were simply re-elected in 1926 and 1928. The Secretary noted the lack of candidates and regretted that no ladies were willing to stand, saying there were several who could fill the position very well. He repeated this at other meetings, but it was not until 1944 that the first two female deacons were elected.

A handful of local women sought an outlet for their talents in missionary work. Maureen Greenwood, of Birchcliffe Baptists, married the Rev K N Wicks and travelled with him to India; Jessie Uttley, also of Birchcliffe, and Miss E A Allsop, of Brearley, both served for decades in Ceylon.

And as women became accustomed to public speaking through the suffrage movement, some names emerged. E.G. Thomas, pastor of Slack chapel, in 1907, civilly mentioned his only female preacher ahead of three young men: "We are pleased to be able to add to the list of our present-day preachers the name of Miss Sarah Speak, of Broadstone – a most capable lady speaker who preaches with unction and power."

But although women's voices are rarely heard, the glimpses we have are in some ways far more revealing than the official picture displayed by the men. Many chapels' records and history booklets (often written for anniversaries) are conscious of their public nature. They speak only respectfully of

Top: A close look at this wedding scene outside Cloughfoot Chapel shows everyone is female, except for one rather grumpy little boy. Presumably a stage play, the date is 1918, were the men absent at war or did the group choose to stay all-female? Picture from the Roger Birch collection, by kind permission of his son.

Above: These ladies have obviously enjoyed sticking on their moustaches to become a dashing pilot and stern barrister in "The Head Butler" a play given at Slack. Back row: Vera Thorpe, Edith Hartley, Annie Redman, Clara Lonsdale. Front row: Annie Speak, Gladys Rawsthorn, Ellen Speak, Ethel Denny. Picture courtesy of Pennine Heritage Digital Archive.

Could we but rule, we'd have a hand in matters
matrimonial,
We'd soon schedule all eligible men, home and
colonial,
On bachelors we'd place a tax, too long they've been
a trifle lax,
Could we but rule.

Chorus—

Oh! shouldn't we be happy, all the men to set
a-quaking,
And wouldn't all old bachelors deep in their shoes be
shaking,
And wouldn't everybody see what wives we would be
making,
Could we but rule.

PART-SONG .... "Oxlips and Violets."

I KNOW a bank whereon the wild thyme blows,
Where oxlips and the nodding violet grows,
There sleeps the Fairy Queen
Sometimes of a night,
Lulled in their flowers
With dances and delight,
I know a bank whereon the wild thyme blows,
Where oxlips and the nodding violet grows.

DIALOGUE .... "Lost! a Collar"

Miss Trinity .... Miss Ellen Winnard.
Cicely, Niece .... Miss A. Cross.
Bertha, ,, ... Miss G. Studd.
Mary, Servant .... Miss A. Lever.
Jane, ,, ... Miss A. Glasse.
Mrs. Crump, Charwoman ... Miss E. Hodgins.

SONG AND CHORUS .... "Skye Boat Song"
(Jacobean Song) .... Miss J. BATTYE.

Chorus—

SPEED, bonnie boat, like a bird on the wing,
Onward! the sailors cry,
Carry the lad that's born to be King
Over the sea to Skye.

Loud the winds howl, loud the waves roar,
Thunder clouds rend the air,
Baffled our foes stand by the hore,
Follow they will not dare.
Speed, bonnie boat, &c.

Though the waves leap, soft shall ye sleep,
Ocean's a Royal bed;
Rocked in the deep, Flora will keep
Watch by your weary head.
Speed, bonnie boat, &c.

Many's the lad fought on that day,
Well the claymore could wield,
When the night came, silently lay
Dead on Culloden's field.
Speed, bonnie boat, &c.

Burned are our homes, exile and death
Scatter the loyal men;
Yet ere the sword cool in the sheath,
Charlie will come again.
Speed, bonnie boat, &c.

CHORUS .... "Animals."

SONG & CHORUS ... "More about Roomfield."

THE men at Roomfield I've heard say
Don't ask ladies to their P.S.A.,
Unless they want one to sing a song,
And that you'll agree with me is wrong.

Chorus—

Ha! ha! ha! P.S.A.,
They don't have ladies there they say,
Except about twice a year or so,
And then they expect us to pay if we go.

Now our young men had an improvement class
To which they would never invite a lass,
And now you see the consequence,
That's gone, with other things, "over the fence."

Chorus—

Ha! ha! ha! P.S.A.,
"Improvement classes," did you say?
There could not very much improvement be
Or ladies would have been invited to see.

In Sunday School they're again behind,
For not one in ten has a strong enough mind
To teach a class of boys, age from six to ten,
So the ladies have to come to the rescue again.

Chorus—

Ha! ha! ha! He! he! he!
How delicate some of them must be,
It's time they interviewed a sage
If they cannot manage boys of that age.

Now our ladies have a different plan,
When they set to work they can beat the men;
They just come to tea every week or so,
And then what happens: Do you know?

Chorus—

Ha! ha! ha! He! he! he!
That's the way at a Ladies' Tea!
Men call it gossip, because you see,
They don't have men at a "Ladies' Tea."

When they come to tea they pay sixpence each,
And use their own provisions as far as they'll reach,
There isn't a better plan in the land
For getting £15 in hand.
Ha! ha! ha! &c.

DOXOLOGY.

Waddingtons, "News" Office, Todmorden.

Above: A programme from a performance at Roomfield Baptist Church, Todmorden, in 1908, by kind permission of Douglas Simpson. The married ladies performed more sedate songs, the above is part of the single ladies' section. Another of their songs was: "Would you know my Celia's charms, Which now excite my fierce alarms? I'm sure she's fortitude and truth, To gain the heart of every youth. She's only thirty lovers now, The rest are gone I can't tell how, No longer Celia ought to strive, For certainly she's fifty-five."

Right: The Birchcliffe Women's Auxiliary Syllabus, 1933-34. Held at the West Yorkshire Archive Service.

founders and donors, singing praises of former members and falling silent on difficulties and disagreements.

Not so the ladies of Roomfield chapel, who would doubtless be amazed that their acid attack on the men's "Pleasant Sunday Afternoons" mutual improvement society would be reprinted more than a century later (pictured left). Who wouldn't want to have been there when they launched into their chorus of disapproval at the men's failure to manage Sunday School classes, refusal to invite lasses to their events and pathetic budgeting? Did the men squirm in their seats, or grin and bear it?

It's certain that Grace Cockcroft never thought her shorthand exercise book would end up wrapped in tissue paper at the West Yorkshire Archive Service, when she ripped the used pages out on August 2, 1932, and started planning her "Pageant of Noble Women", for performance at Birchcliffe Baptist Chapel (see overleaf).

And it seems unlikely that the conscientious notetaker of the Yorkshire Association of Baptist Churches' catering committee (Hope Church), thought she was writing for posterity when she recorded the 26 dozen table knives and forks and 3 dozen sugar tongs needed for a post-service luncheon on Tuesday following Whit Monday, 1911: "There was far too much white bread. The loaves provided weighed about 7lb each and 45 of these would have been enough."

But these rare glimpses perhaps show us more of life in the church than pages of dry minutes of texts of sermons. They may have been unacclaimed, but they certainly seem as capable, outspoken and strong-minded as we would expect Northern women to be.

SYLLABUS.

1933-1934.

Apl. 11	Meeting.
May 9 ... ... "My Picture Gallery" Mrs. Knight, Hebden Bridge.	
June 13 ...	Ladies' Trip to Scarborough.
,, 20	Open Meeting.
,, 24	Garden Party. Mr. and Mrs. C. Thomas, Hazelwood.
July 11 ... ... "Canadian Ranch Life." Mrs. Blosse, Hebden Bridge.	
Aug. 8	Meeting. Miss Thorpe, Halifax.
,, 19	Garden Party. Mr. Newton Greenwood, (Arnsbrae.)
Sep. 12 "The work of the Dr. Barnardo's Homes." Miss Wilkins, Rochdale.	

SYLLABUS.—(Continued.)

Oct. 10 "My visit to the United States." Miss A. Eastwood, Golcar.	
Nov. 14	Meeting.
,, 18—19	Ladies' Week-end.
,, 21	Lantern Lecture. Coun. E. B. Gibson, Hebden Bridge.
Dec. 12 ... "Recitals Grave and Gay." Mrs. Hanson, Elland.	
1934 Jan. 9	Meeting. Mrs. Westlake, Luddendenfoot.
,, 23 Lantern Lecture. "Hills and Dales of Derbyshire." Coun. Sam Greenwood. Wadsworth.	
Feb. 13	Shrovetide Event.
Feb. 27 "Human welfare and the League." Miss Warburton, Mytholmroyd.	
Mar. 13	Annual Meeting.

Recital   Mrs John Eastwood
Introduction   Mrs G. B. Gibson
Spirit of the ages   Miss D Crabtree
   Dreamer   Miss P. Thomas
              Group 1   Bible Characters
Miriam   Mrs C. Lomas

Deborah   Mrs Fred Greenwood

Ruth   Miss Dora Greenwood
Naomi
Sister in law   Mrs J. T Dewhirst
A Woman of Samaria   Mrs Lingard

Lydia   Miss Edith Greenwood
                         (Eiffel St.

Notes for "A Pageant of Noble Women " performed by Birchcliffe ladies in 1932 - and what a celebration of intelligence and commitment it is! In contrast to most of today's power lists, there is not a single entertainer of any kind, with the possible exception of Charlotte Bronte, who comes under "Emancipators of Women". The only other novelist is Harriet Beecherstow, who really wrote as a way of promoting the abolition of slavery.

Many are campaigners for women's rights, though the Pankhursts have been snubbed even though they had visited Hebden Bridge (at the time, many considered their methods too violent). Not one has been included for her beauty or wealth, the only possible touch of self-indulgence coming from poet Elizabeth Browning.

Perhaps most startling is the "Bible Characters" group, which contains none of the usual female characters: Mary and Martha, the sisters who listened to Jesus speak and cooked his dinner have been left out, as have the repentant prostitute Mary Magdalene and the Virgin Mary. Instead, there's an implied argument for sexual freedom. Grace Cockcroft, your daughters salute you. All spellings are as written, annotations in brackets are mine.

Group 1: Bible Characters: Miriam (Aaron's sister, a prophetess), Deborah (a warlike prophetess who led an Israeli army after its general refused to go to war without her), Ruth and Naomi (a devoted mother- and daughter-in-law who are often used as an emblem of sisterhood), A Woman of Samaria, Lydia (a wealthy trader who was converted by Paul).

The inclusion of the Woman of Samaria as a noble woman is the most controversial. Jesus asked the Woman of Samaria to draw him a drink of water. The story continues: 'Jesus said to her, "Go, call your husband, and come here." The woman answered him, "I have no husband." Jesus said to her,"You are right in saying, 'I have no husband'; for you have had five husbands, and the one you now have is not your husband. What you have said is true." The woman said to him, "Sir, I perceive that you are a prophet."' The woman later told the townspeople: "Come, see a man who told me all that I ever did. Can this be the Christ?" As a result, many believed in him. It is not written in the Bible that Jesus asked her to seek forgiveness for her life of sin, or that she ever did so. Mr Lingard's reaction to his wife's role is not recorded.

Group 2: Champions of Freedom and Liberty: Bodicea, Margaret Wilson (possibly the US First Lady Margaret Woodrow Wilson), Madame Rowland (a political activist of the French revolution), Lady Jane Grey (one of the most learned women of her day, she was nominated to the throne by her cousin, Edward VI, but beheaded for treason by Mary), Dr Elsie Engliss (a Scottish doctor and suffragist), Harriet Beecherstow (author of Uncle Tom's Cabin, credited with having sparked the American Civil War).

Group 3: Pioneers of Christianity and spreaders of Life and Truth: Bertha Queen of Kent (Saint Aldeburgh), Genevieve (saved Paris from Attila the Hun), Susannah Wesley (mother of the Wesleys), Katherine Booth (the "mother" of the Salvation Army), Monica (mother of Saint Augustine), Mary Slesser (a missionary to Nigeria who promoted women's rights).

Group 4: Emancipators of Women: Hypatia (a Greek philosopher and mathematician), St Cecelia (patron saint of music, she refused to marry), Charlotte Bronte, Mary Somerville (a science writer), Harriet Martineau (a sociologist and politician)

Group 5: Women of Great Renown: Queen Elizabeth, Joan of Arc, Frances R Havergal (a religious poet and hymn writer), Elizabeth Browning, Helen Keller (a deaf-blind American author, political activist and lecturer), Frances Willard (an American educator, temperance reformer and women's suffragist).

Chapter Eight
The Fall of Zion

When the last great building project of the movement began on Foster Lane's twin onion domes in Hebden Bridge, 1904, (pictured page 24) the centrality of the chapel in valley life must have seemed unshakeable. It seems incredible that it could fall away so quickly. How did it happen?

Like all churches, the Great War took a heavy toll on the young of the chapels, the lifeblood that gave zest to all its work and entertainments. A moving entry in the annual reports of Todmorden's Roomfield Baptist Chapel in 1917 reads: "At the present time we are living, as it were, under a cloud – the dark cloud of war; and this is having a sad effect on the work of our church. About 90 of our young men have left us, serving King and Country in various ways. Some have given their lives, some have been wounded, and others are still doing their share in this great but awful conflict. As a church, we miss these boys very much, and we hope and pray that the time will soon come when they can come back to us again."

For those who remained, life was suspended, the busy round of bazaars, concerts and picnics losing their point when so many were missing. The romances that had flowered behind the scenes were all on hold.

Opposite page: This memorial, based on photographs, shows all the men who served from Vale Baptist Church. The centre 16 were killed.

Bridge Street chapel, known as a cathedral of Methodism, was a worthy neighbour to Todmorden Town Hall. These pictures, from the Roger Birch collection by permission of his son, show the demolition in 1962. A rather grim supermarket now stands on the site.

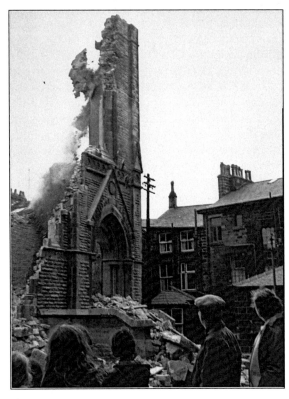

Even with the end of the war, there was change. State education was now firmly embedded, and replaced much of the need for Sunday Schools. More varied entertainments, cinemas and cheaper travel, drew people away from the fruit teas and lantern lectures. Even the more comfortable, well-lit homes with central heating must have made draughty lecture rooms less attractive.

They had also lost their driving purpose. Their causes - universal suffrage, education, trade unions - were now accepted by all parties. Like the Green Party today, their own success had made them redundant.

As mills closed, millowners' patriarchy crumbled and congregations dwindled, the true scale of the over-supply of chapels in the valley became apparent. Caring for the vanity projects of the past was soon far beyond the means of tiny, elderly groups and, in unheated buildings, the great enemy, dry rot, always lurked above.

For most chapels, the downward trajectory was inevitable, though rarely chronicled. Narrating the rise of the movement is fairly straightforward – detailed records were kept of stone-layings and opening ceremonies by a proud and happy people. Researching its last days is harder. Records fall silent, even the dates of final services are sometimes uncertain.

One of the saddest closures was of Booth's "miniature cathedral". The elderly ladies remaining were under such stress at attempting to maintain it that when they applied for demolition, the sympathetic local conservation group decided it would be a cruelty to force them to keep it by having it designated a listed building.

Dick Eccles, of Hebden Bridge's Zion Chapel, which was not paid for by millowners, felt free to speak his mind in his "Song of Zion" as most official chapel historians did not.

"The scourge of many nonconformist and free-church chapels in the north of England at this period is that they were sponsored by wealthy mill-owners. There was a tendency for these men to try to out-do their business rivals by building larger and more ornate chapels than they had done. They also made it a condition of employment at their mills that the workers should attend... this was an extremely short-sighted policy. This is not the way to fill chapels! These activities are a millstone round the neck of nonconformists all over the north of England, an unfortunate episode from which nonconformity has never recovered."

Not all closed without a fight. At this same modest "Strict and Particular" Baptist chapel, one extraordinarily ordinary woman decided not to give in. Florence Walton had joined in 1912 at 15 and had worked all her life in a mill. She watched the gradual decline of her chapel, frequently being the only person to turn up for worship, until, in 1963, she found herself the only remaining member.

Yet she decided that, if God had led his people to build it in 1881, she would need a clear indication from him that he wanted it closed. Until then, for years, she went alone every Sunday morning to read her Bible, pray and sometimes sing hymns. One of her problems was that she could not draw on chapel funds, because the bank required the signatures of two members for any transaction. When she considered the chapel needed redecorating, she had to draw on her own savings.

Florrie Walton and the interior of the Mount Zion Chapel, Osborne Street, Hebden Bridge, where she worshipped alone for so long. The text reads: "One Lord, One Faith, One Baptism". Both pictures courtesy of the current pastor Luke Jenner.

One Sunday morning, she read in her Bible "Is it time for you to dwell in your ceiled houses, and this house lie waste?" (Haggai 1:4). She had recently installed electricity in her own house, and took this as a sign that she should also do so for the chapel, which was still lit by gas. The next morning, she made arrangements for electric power and lights in the chapel.

Still, Florrie knew a well-maintained building wasn't enough. A church needs a minister, so she invited Irishman Dick Eccles, quoted above, to join her. His friends teased him "If you split that church, you'll be had up for manslaughter," but in 1969 he moved into one of the underdwellings beneath the chapel. Within a few years, through evangelism and a new Sunday school, he built the membership up again. Florrie enthusiastically accepted his changes, such as a new hymn book, and present members remember her gamely clambering over stiles to join the young people on camping holidays.

Cross Lanes Chapel, halfway up the hill to Heptonstall, was gutted by fire and demolished to make way for a bungalow. The graveyard can still be seen at the top of the Buttress. Picture by Jack Uttley, by kind permission of his son.

She died in 1980, aged 83. The church continued to grow, with many members travelling from Halifax, so a few years ago it was decided to build new premises in Pellon, including rooms for a baby and toddler group and other facilities. The old building was not demolished, but was converted into flats, and Florrie is still remembered with gratitude and love.

Happy endings, though rare, are not impossible. Hebden Bridge's classical Hope Baptist Church gave their neighbouring Sunday School to the council, and it is now a friendly and light-filled library. The main chapel, having been refused permission to convert into social housing because of a lack of parking, recently received a major grant for renovation and is still operating. Above it on the hillside, Birchcliffe has been imaginatively converted into a stunning arts and community centre.

But for the most part the regular closures and demolitions through the 1960s and 1970s went almost unchallenged, with no more than a short valedictory and a dramatic picture of the demolition in the local paper.

The process of closing them was, and still is, fairly straightforward: perhaps too straightforward. Unlike the Church of England, with its baroque procedures and layers of authority that must be consulted before a church is closed, the non-conformists were free to act at local level.

Even now, some of the last remnants are disappearing. Walsden is closed and up for sale. Old Town, with its curving exterior staircase, held its last service in August 2013. The lovely landmark of Lumbutts, home to the

Top: the original interior of Birchcliffe, Hebden Bridge. Built to seat 1,017, it was really too big for any purpose although the basement was used as a restaurant and the back Sunday School as a hostel.

Above: It was imaginatively remodelled by creating a new floor at the gallery level, producing a superb auditorium above and a suite of offices beneath. All pictures courtesy of the Pennine Horizons Digital Archive.

stained glass of several closed churches and a three-tonne organ, is due to hold its last service before the end of 2013.

Having dominated the valley for over a century, it seems incredible that so many of these monuments to hard work and a belief in self-improvement could disappear in a few short decades. Having been so all-encompassing, it has left barely a trace on our history or collective mind. Many who live in the valley today, though still valuing the very traits of independence of thought and action that created non-conformism, have never heard of it.

Part of this, as stated earlier, was due to the snobbish attitude of the establishment and the continued influence of their propaganda, but it was partly due to the non-conformists themselves. They were a practical people, and had not produced the art that informs national consciousness. Their books of sermons, so debated at the time, could never survive the way literature does, and they had dismissed as heretical the statues and religious paintings that still have pride of place in galleries.

Their major physical legacy was their architecture, and this had been derided from the start. In the North, the very ubiquity of the village chapel also meant that their simple and graceful lines were undervalued.

Most books of this kind, like most of the chapel history booklets on which this has drawn, close with an exhortation to further works, or at least to value what is left. It is impossible to turn the clock back, and much of what was once a public blessing is gone or in private hands. We cannot all help to conserve the remains, but we can at least be grateful to those who built so much, not just the characteristic buildings that dot our landscapes, but also the social justice, universal education and workers' rights that we all enjoy every day. The dissenters' contribution to all our freedoms cannot be overestimated. In the words of the Sowerby historian W.H. Leah:

> "And what shall we more say? Time would fail us to tell of the Abrahams, Isaacs and Jacobs, the Josephs and Benjamins, the James Johns and Philips, and others perhaps not less saintly the Williams, the Charles, the Sutcliffes; also the Hannahs, the Elizabeths, and the Marys, the Sarahs, and many others too numerous to mention, who, through faith and patience, now inherit the promised Kingdom of God."

Part Two

Tracking down
our legacies

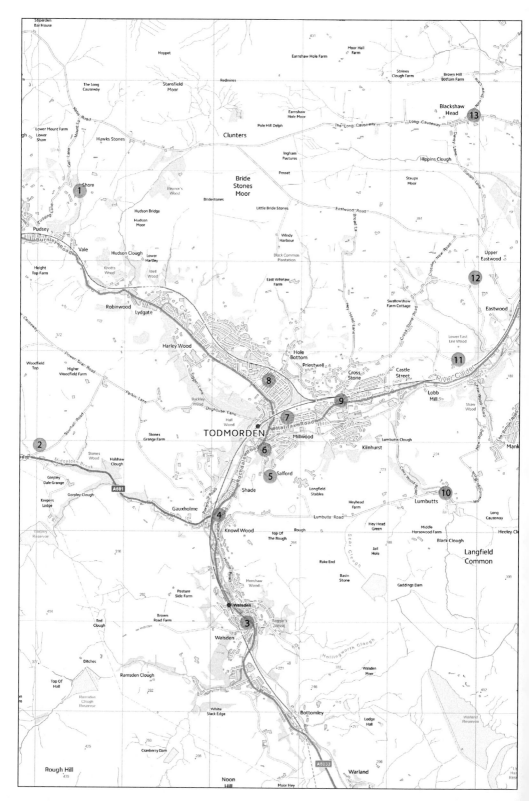

More than 100 chapels have been built in the valley, but most have now disappeared. In the 19th century many were demolished to make way for grander buildings, in the 20th century to make way for bungalows and supermarkets. Others have been altered beyond all recognition and so are not included here. However, there are still plenty worth a look, and a selection are given here. For zoomable maps and a fuller list, including more pictures of the lost chapels, visit chapelvalley.org.uk.

1. Shore (pictured above, by Roger Birch) Once a major landmark standing proud on the hillside, with daughter churches in Cornholme and Todmorden, it was reluctantly abandoned by the remaining small congregation when the roof fell in and repairs proved too expensive. It was sold into private hands, and, though in residential use, is still largely derelict. Only the unprepossessing back can be seen if approached from the village of Shore, it is best seen from the footpath at the back.

2. Cloughfoot chapel and Sunday school. See front cover for picture. The Sunday School is a long low building on the main road, built in 1829 and marked by a plaque on the gable end. The chapel was built later in 1854, higher on the hillside up a short lane opposite the school.

3. Walsden. The congregation here was an amalgamation, partly from Thornsgreese, high up on the moors above it and now a private house (the word "greese" means steep steps). A former chapel in the valley bottom was replaced with this building in 1861, with the date plaque from the original. It was closed in 2010 and, at time of writing, was on sale with its interior intact.

4. Shade. This pleasant, substantial chapel, built in 1848, is easily seen from the road and is now private flats.

5. Quaker graveyard. From the Unitarian Church, walk up Shoebroad Lane between fields. A plaque next to the gates marks the graveyard where the lane bends sharply round a clump of trees. The Society of Friends, which cares for the spot, are happy for it to be used for picnics if walkers clear away their rubbish.

6 Todmorden Unitarian Church, former chapel and Quaker chapel. No tour would be complete without a look at the Grade 1 listed Unitarian Church, see interior picture on page 21. It was paid for by the three Fielden brothers in memory of their father and designed by John Gibson, a distinguished London architect who had already worked for the Fieldens. At the same time Gibson built Dobroyd Castle for the middle brother John, positioned so that Castle and Church could be seen from each other. Gibson followed this magnificent double by building the neo-classical Todmorden Town Hall. After suffering vandalism and decay, the church was acquired by the Historic Chapels Trust and can be hired for events.

The original chapel is also still standing a little further along the road and marked by a plaque which can be seen from steps leading down to the back of the former Golden Lion pub. It is now flats.

Less obviously a religious building is the Quaker meeting house, a square built house behind a wall opposite the gates at the back of the Unitarian Church, next to the Honey Hole road sign. It is unmarked, but can be identified by its central arched doorway and two chimneys.

7. Central Street, Todmorden (pictured above). This is all that is left of Todmorden's many splendid Methodist buildings. After the demolition of the main chapels of York Street, Bridge Street and Patmos, the Methodist congregations amalgamated in to the York Street Sunday School, renamed as Central Methodist Church. The roofline was altered but the splendid central windows were preserved. This is still a well-used building by several local groups and is open to the public.

8 . Victoria Road primitive methodists (pictured below, from the Roger Birch collection) is now the St John Ambulance station, although its attractive arched window has been replaced.

9. Millwood, Todmorden. Pictured on page 24. Now barely recognisable due to a front extension, but easily spotted on the main road as Leah's Pet Foods. The original name "Rehoboth" is carved over the door.

10. Lumbutts (pictured below, from the Roger Birch collection). The steep-pitched roof of Lumbutts is visible from miles across the moors. Although its afternoon teas were popular with walkers, at time of writing, it was due to be closed. It contains the stained glass from the nearby demolished church of Mankinholes.

11 and 12. Rodwell End and Benthead. Two of the original chapels described and pictured in chapter 1. Both are along narrow lanes with private parking only, and are best approached on foot. At Benthead, the path goes past the gable end of the building and to the back, from where the original window can be seen in the opposite gable end.

13. Blackshaw Head. Built on a former bull-baiting ring in 1815 as an offshoot from Heptonstall, it is still in use as a chapel and community centre.

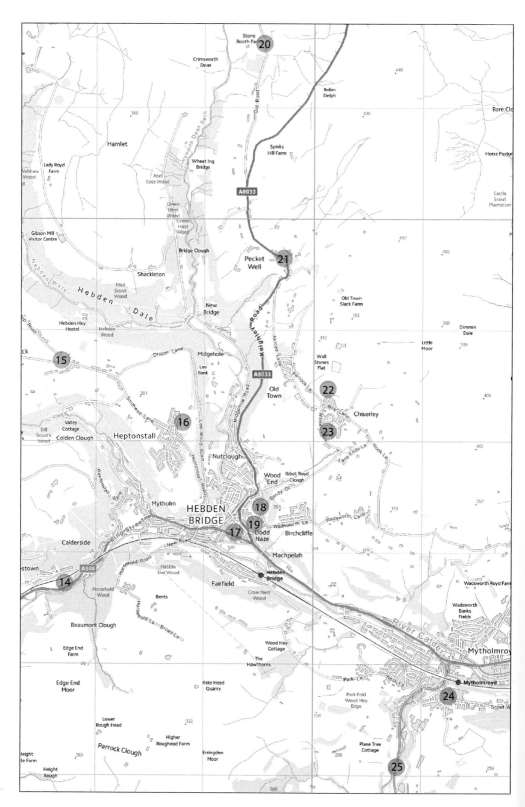

14. Nazebottom (pictured below, from the Roger Birch collection) This was the last chapel springing from the Benthead congregation. They first moved to "Old Naze" higher up the hillside in 1846, the graveyard can still be seen just off the Pennine Way near Higher Underbank Farm. The congregation later bought this site just above the main road, opening the new chapel and Sunday School in 1912. The building had some alterations when turned into private housing but can still be recognised.

15. Robertshaws/Slack. Pictured on pages 11 and 17, old and new buildings are both easily seen from the road. The new building is undergoing renovation by the evangelical group which now owns it.

16. Heptonstall Octagon. Pictured on page 13, this is a must-see. Although tucked away down a flight of stairs off Northgate, it is usually open to the public.

17. Hope, Hebden Bridge. Old and new buildings are pictured on page 16, and the interiors of both can be seen. The original Ebenezer building, which sat 500-plus, is now the Heart Gallery with flats above. The classical new building, facing the cinema, will re-open to the public after renovation work.

18. Birchcliffe, Hebden Bridge. Pictured on page 77, this is a re-purposing success story. It is regularly open to the public and can be hired for parties. The former Sunday School behind it is a hostel.

19 . Mount Zion, Hebden Bridge. Pictured on page 75, this is now private housing on the over- and under-dwelling pattern. From Osborne Street, it seems a modest building. Its rear arched windows are best admired from across the park, or from the pay and display car park off Albert Street.

20. Crimsworth Dean (pictured below, from the Jack Uttley collection). Despite the tiny size of the chapel, the Crimsworth Dean congregation was one of the oldest when their "new" chapel finally closed in 1996. It started as one of the Darney Societies, being located on what was then the main road from Haworth to Heptonstall, which John Wesley and the Haworth preacher William Grimshaw travelled many times. The group originally met in the kitchens of Handibutt Farm, then Cross Ends Farm. Sometimes known as T' New School and sometimes as the School at Top O' T' Loin, it was built in 1865 and cost £500, with stone from Delph End Quarry. Though initially popular, handloom weaving was already in decline and the area emptied as people left for work in the mills. Haworth New Road meant traffic passed Crimsworth Dean by, and when it closed in 1996 it had only four regular attenders. The last steward, Carl Wilson, described the spot as being so peaceful as to have "magical qualities".

21 Crimsworth, Pecket Well. Chapel and Sunday School face each other across the main road, both are now private housing. The chapel was described as "delightfully upspoilt" by architectural historian Christopher Stell, who wrote of its classical elements: "A moulded cornice runs boldly across the front gable, the doorway has a small pediment with eared ends, and a tablet in the main gable is set in an architectural frame".

22 Wainsgate. Now owned by the Historic Chapels Trust, it is cared for by the Friends of Wainsgate and is still open to the public for concerts and heritage days, when the beautifully unspoilt interior can be viewed. The Sunday School is used as artists' studios. John Fawcett is buried in its atmospheric graveyard. Well worth a visit.

23 Old Town. Closed as a chapel in August 2013, this typical model of Sunday School below and chapel above was once a thriving community organisation with a large lending library. Its curving exterior staircase has proved a challenge to undertakers over the years.

24 Mytholmroyd. This picture, from the Jack Uttley collection, shows the 1826 broad-fronted chapel on the left and the attached 1872 Sunday School on the right. The Georgian chapel collapsed in 1979 and, despite opposition from conservationists, it was demolished. Worship was transferred to the Sunday School building. It has since been fully modernised and is well used.

25 Cragg Vale. This simple chapel was built in 1855 and closed in 1970. It is now a private house. Travel two miles out of Mytholmroyd, and it is on the right hand side with its gable end facing the road.

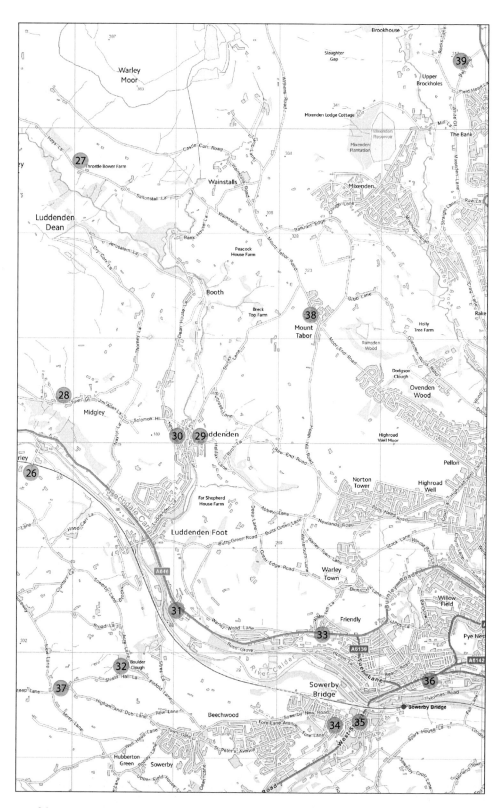

26. Brearley. The Brearley congregation was an off-shoot from Ebenezer, Hebden Bridge, formed by members of the Fawcett family and others. Their first building (pictured below, from the Jack Uttley collection) built in 1845 was named Bethel, but was locally known as "Little Faith", because it was designed to be easily converted to a row of cottages should the mission fail. In fact, it succeeded beyond all expectation and was soon too small. A new site across the field was used in 1875 to build the new chapel, Sunday School and manse (pictured bottom, courtesy of Tim Green), all now in residential use. The original building has since had an extension built across the walled-up arch doorway, but can still be recognised at right-angles to the lane, facing its grand successor.

27. Luddenden Dean graveyard. The chapel was built in 1821 and destroyed by fire in 1954. Though the fire brigade attended, the only water was from springs and the building was gutted. However, the "orphans' grave" can still be seen in the churchyard. This is a monument to seven girls, aged 12 and 17, who died while working in Calvert's mill, Wainstalls. Many orphans were employed there, mostly brought from the workhouses in Liverpool. By modern standards they would be considered to be virtually slaves.

28. Midgley. This was the second Midgley chapel. Class meetings were held in the village for many years before the first square-built chapel with a sanded stone floor and whitewashed walls was built in 1819. It was replaced with the present building in 1883 and is now private housing.

29. United Methodist Free, Luddenden, and 30, St James United Luddenden. Standing on opposite sides of the valley, these two churches are both now private housing. The United Methodist Free Church, built in 1837 is an unusual shape. It was designed with cottages underneath on to the High Street, a Sunday School above it and the chapel, overlooking the Sunday School, on top. The chapel had a horseshoe shaped gallery with a pulpit and organ connecting the two ends. St James' United was built in 1902 as its larger replacement. It closed in 2012.

31 Luddenden Foot United Reformed Church. A landmark on the main Halifax Road, the clock tower makes it easy to spot. Pictured on page 18. The intrepid may like to climb the stone steps set into the wall by the bus stop opposite it. At the top, are the remains of Luddenden Foot Methodist Church and its overgrown graveyard.

32. Boulder Clough. Picture above courtesy of Tim Green. Unlike any other chapel in the area, this was designed in the Arts and Crafts style with conical towers and an internal arrangement shaped like a Greek cross. It opened in 1898 and became known as the Ranters' Chapel, due to the lively debates of the Mutual Improvement Society, which was known for its quick repartee and sometimes rowdy responses. It was also home to the celebrated "Ancient Order of Henpecked Husbands", which started as a rambling society of six Methodist preachers who met on Easter Mondays in the 1890s. They later moved their jovial meetings to Boulder Clough, eventually disbanding in the 1970s. A full and funny account by local historian John Kerridge is on www.sowerbytown.org.uk.

33 Friendly. Two former chapels sit on either side of Halifax Road near its junction with Tuel Lane. The larger, built in 1890 and now a furniture showroom, is easy to spot, although the tops of its arched windows have been filled in. The other is less obvious, standing at the junction with Water Hill Lane, and now home to the Friendly Brass Band. The ground floor was single-storey dwellings, the top floor was a simple chapel.

34 Quaker Meeting House, Sowerby Street, Sowerby Bridge. Described and pictured in chapter 1. Now a private house, it is a little decrepit but still likely to last another 200 years.

35 Sowerby Bridge Wesleyan Mission Chapel. Built 1890, it looks a little austere thanks to its narrow windows, but its practical size and design mean it is still in use as a youth and community centre.

36 Bolton Brow, Sowerby Bridge. This enormous chapel was built in 1832 with typical nonconformist practicality to include warehouses for the canal on the ground floor at the back. It has had various uses and has now been converted to flats.

37 Steep Lane, Sowerby. This Baptist church has been rebuilt twice since its first inception in 1751. This building opened in 1875. The congregation was faced with serious structural problems in 1986, and decided to demolish the upper chapel storey and re-build the pediment over the lower floor. The result is a more practically-sized chapel which is still in use.

38 Mount Tabor. This Grade 2 listed chapel, sitting 1,000ft above sea level, was built in 1820 by local men who worked for free. It is still in use with a small congregation and well-used community rooms, this chapel was known for its generous teas and celebrations.

39. Mount Zion, Upper Brockholes. Picture below courtesy of Tim Green. Although a little way out of the Upper Calder Valley, this is one of the most attractive Georgian chapels. John Wesley preached in the earlier buildings of 1773, recording it as "standing alone in a dreary waste". The current buildings date from 1815, but include the date stone and sundial from the original. The chapel houses a collection of ceramics and the cottage where Wesley stayed can still be used for retreats and meetings.

Reading a Chapel

From the outside, the first thing to note is chapels are usually built square to the road. As God is everywhere, dissenters believed orienting a church to the East was superstition. Chapels can show a splendid face to the front.

Inside, there is no altar. There may be a small wooden communion table, but chapels are designed for teaching, not ritual, so pride of place is given to the pulpit, which may have two or even three levels. It is commonly raised so the preacher can be clearly heard in the galleries, which were part of the design for the same reason, to bring a larger audience closer to the speaker. There may be more forward-facing seats below the pulpit for officials. Music was also central so choir or orchestra galleries face the congregation. Chapel interiors were often re-arranged to give organs due prominence.

Early chapels had forms to sit on, but these were usually replaced with box pews. Kneelers are not included, as it was not considered necessary to kneel to pray. During prayer, the congregation sometimes turned around in their pews and stood with their backs to the minister.

Chapels rarely have statues or paintings, as these were corrupt symbols of idolatry. Instead, texts were painted on walls as at Heptonstall octagon, pictured here, reading "Mine house shall be called a house of prayer for all people" and "I was glad when they said unto me let us go into the house of the Lord".

Stained glass windows were also rarely installed in older chapels, as they were both too expensive and too reminiscent of a traditional church. As time went by and the non-conformists gained confidence and money, they were sometimes added. Later dissident chapels have some splendid examples, such as the Todmorden Unitarian Church.

Bethels and Ebenezers

Non-conformists held that worship belonged only to the Trinity, so chapels are rarely named for saints. Most were unpretentiously given local names, but some have a significance that is lost in a secular age. Common names include:

Ebenezer, meaning Stone of Help. This was set up by Samuel to commemorate God's help of Israel in the battle against the Philistines. (1 Samuel 7:7-12)

Bethel, meaning House of God. At Bethel God spoke to the people of Israel. First mentioned in Genesis 28:10, when Jacob has a vision of angels ascending and descending a ladder reaching up to heaven. He returned to the place 'built an altar, and called the place El-beth-el'. Later, the Ark of the Covenant was kept at Bethel (20:26-28). The people of Israel visited and received instruction from God in difficult times. Samuel held his court of justice there (1 Samuel 7:16).

Mount Tabor. This mountain in Israel is believed to the site of the Transfiguration of Jesus. Jesus ascended a mountain to pray with Peter, John and James. As he prayed, 'his raiment became dazzling white' and Moses and Elijah appeared to speak to him (Matthew 17:1–9, Mark 9:2-8, Luke 9:28–36).

Below: Ebenezer Chapel, Luddenden, is the plain building on the right, the fancier Sunday school is on the left.

Mount Olivet. The Mount of Olives is close to Jerusalem and is frequently mentioned in the New Testament. Here, Jesus taught and prophesied to his disciples (Matthew 24-25), speaking of the end of times. After the Last Supper, Jesus and the disciples went and sang on Mount Olivet; the Garden of Gethsemane, where Jesus was betrayed, is at its foot (Matthew 26:30). After the resurrection, Jesus ascended into heaven from here (Acts 1:9-13).

Mount Zion. This term is sometimes used for Israel, and the frequent use of the name reflects the belief that Christians are God's new chosen people. It is a hill in Jerusalem just outside the walls of the Old City. It is frequently mentioned in the Bible as 'a stronghold of Zion', the site of King David's palace.

Tin Tabernacle. This quirky name for the pre-fabricated chapels is particularly apt, as the Tabernacle was a portable dwelling place of God during the Exodus. It was built to divinely-revealed specifications and is thought to have been a tent-sanctuary, housing the Ark of the Covenant, (Exodus 25:8-9)

Providence. The term providence has been debased to mean little more than good luck, but in theology providence is God's intervention in the world. A distinction is usually made between "general providence", which refers to God's continuous upholding of the existence and natural order of the universe, and "special providence", which refers to God's extraordinary intervention in the lives of people.

Salem: This town is referred to at least twice in the Bible, including Psalm 76:1-2, "God is renowned in Judah; in Israel his name is great. His tent is in Salem, his dwelling place in Zion". Various towns have been named for it, the most notorious being Salem, New England, scene of the witch trials.

Sources

Any project like this relies on the diarists, chroniclers and just plain hoarders who have saved programmes, kept minutes and recorded memories for generations. Thank you to all of them.

Anonymous, *The Beginning of Association life in Yorkshire and Lancashire*, from the Baptist Quarterly

Anonymous *Centenary Vale Baptist Church*

Anonymous *Salem Wesleyan Church, Hebden Bridge*

Anonymous *Todmorden Unitarian Church*

Anonymous *Rules for the management of the Methodist Sunday School*

Anonymous *Wadsworth and Crimsworth Dean, past and present.*

Alternative Technology Centre *Power in the Landscape*

Chapman, E.V., and Turner, Gordon, *History of Heptonstall Chapel*

Collinge, Rodney, *Non-conformist Chapels of Luddenden Valley*

Crabtree, Lewis *A Review of Methodism at Old Town*

Eccles, Dick *Song of Zion*

Hargreaves, John A *'Suffer the Children': Methodist Attitudes to Education and Youth in Halifax, 1800-2000*; *Benjamin Rushton, Handloom Weaver, Radical Agitator and Nonconformist Preacher*; *Edwardian Decline: Baptists and Congregationalists in Halifax and its Hinterland*; and *Methodist Growth and Secession in the Parish of Halifax 1740 - 1851*, all in the Transactions of the Halifax Antiquarian Society

Jennings, Bernard, editor, and contributors from the Hebden Bridge WEA *Pennine Valley*; and *History of Todmorden*

Leah, W.H. *A brief historical sketch of the Congregational Church at Sowerby*

McLeod, Hugh, Chapter 30 of *Atlas of Industrialising Britain*

Neave, David and Susan *East Riding Chapels and Meeting Houses*

Powell, Ken *The Fall of Zion*

Simpson, Douglas *Roomfield Baptist Church, A brief history*

Stell, Christopher *Calderdale Chapels*, Transactions of the Halifax Antiquarian Society

Taylor, Adam *Memoirs of the Rev. Dan Taylor*

Thomas, E.G. *Centenary Souvenir Heptonstall Slack Baptist Church*

Thompson, E.P. *The Making of the English Working Class*

Thomson, Charles W *Wainsgate Baptist Chapel West Yorkshire*

Wilson, Benjamin, *Struggles of an Old Chartist*

Wilson, Rev W B, and Davies, Rev W B, *A History of the Halifax and Calder Valley District of Baptist Churches*

Young, Kenneth, *Chapel*

Apart from those named in picture credits, thanks are also due to Daniel Birch, Kath Lawson, Gerard Liston, Keith Stansfield, John Uttley, Frank Woolrych, and the staff of Hebden Bridge Library and the West Yorkshire Archive Service.

Particular thanks are due to the following:

Jack Uttley (1914 - 2003) was born in Heptonstall and lived in the upper Calder Valley for all his life. He was locally well known as a photographer and local historian. He was instrumental in setting up both the Hebden Bridge and the Mytholmroyd History Societies.

Roger Birch (1941 - 2013) was born in Todmorden. He was a lecturer in graphic design and photography, and exhibited his own work throughout the country. He was also a collector of some 4,000 historic pictures and is best known for his "Todmorden Album" series.

Rodney Collinge has done much valuable work as a historian and is now honorary president of the Luddenden Conservation Society. He advised on this book and kindly shared some of the images from his own work, pictured left.

Ann Kilbey is co-author of "City in the Hills", about the building of the Walshaw Dean reservoirs, pictured right. She has done a great deal of work with Frank Woolrych and others on the Pennine Heritage Digital Archive, and sourced many images for this book.

Many thanks also to the ladies of the Heptonstall Methodist Chapel, whose work over the decades to maintain their heritage started this project.